Agile Security Operations

Engineering for agility in cyber defense, detection, and response

Hinne Hettema

BIRMINGHAM—MUMBAI

Agile Security Operations

Group Product Manager: Wilson Dsouza
Publishing Product Manager: Vijin Boricha
Senior Editor: Arun Nadar
Content Development Editor: Sulagna Mohanty
Technical Editor: Arjun Varma
Copy Editor: Safis Editing
Project Coordinator: Shagun Saini
Proofreader: Safis Editing
Indexer: Subalakshmi Govindhan
Production Designer: Jyoti Chauhan

First published: February 2022

Production reference: 1141221

Published by Packt Publishing Ltd.
Livery Place
35 Livery Street
Birmingham
B3 2PB, UK.

ISBN 978-1-80181-551-2

www.packt.com

To all my teachers on the path.

– Hinne Hettema

Contributors

About the author

Hinne Hettema is a practitioner in cybersecurity operations, focusing especially on enabling security capabilities through detection engineering, security monitoring, threat intelligence, incident response, operational technology, and malware research. He works in New Zealand in security operations and the establishment of cybersecurity defensive capabilities in various organizations. He is an adjunct senior fellow at the University of Queensland, researching cybersecurity operations, the security of operational technology, and the philosophy of cybersecurity. He studied theoretical chemistry and philosophy.

About the reviewers

Rene Thorup holds an MSc degree in forensic computing with distinction and a Dean's award from Coventry University and an academic profession degree in IT networks and electronics technology. He has over 20 years' experience within cybersecurity, from cybersecurity analyst to CISO, and he has even been a university lecturer and cybersecurity trainer for a leading incident response company. Rene has built, and led, several SOC and SecOps teams from scratch over the years, both for the military/governments and large enterprises. Recently, he was the technical lead for EMEA and APAC for a well-known cybersecurity firm, and conducted incident response and root cause analysis on several high-profile cyber-attacks.

> *I would like to thank the professional leaders that always believed in me and my abilities to succeed and supported my continuous development – especially "PT" and "MF" from the Danish Defense. Also, a big thanks to "Lex," who was a great inspiration for keeping up the hard study on my MSc, and made it fun to study.*

Beshoy A. Iskander holds two MSc degrees in cybersecurity and technology management and holds other professional certifications in cyber security and incident response, with 15 years of experience in cyber security across multiple security vendors, such as RSA and other firms in the FinTech industry.

Currently, Beshoy is the director of cyber security operations for a multinational crypto-currency company.

> *I would like to thank God first, for his grace, which led me to this point in my life. I'd also like to thank my wife, Lidia; my first son, Jonathan; my second child to be; and my mother. I'd also love to dedicate my contribution to this book to the soul of my father.*

Table of Contents

3

Engineering for Incident Response

Section 2: Defensible Organizations

4

Key Concepts in Cyber Defense

7
How Secure Are You? – Measuring Security Posture

Section 3: Advanced Agile Security Operations

8
Red, Blue, and Purple Teaming

Appendix
Further reading

Index
Other Books You May Enjoy

Preface

This book focuses on how organizations can improve their security posture and build robust and predictable security operations. It is written from the viewpoint that the best way to do that is with something called *agile security operations*, focused on *processes* rather than organizational *structure*, and a strong focus on incident response as one of the key processes that we either prepare for, execute, or improve in well-executed security operations.

This book may turn some received wisdom about security operations on its head. Specifically, in this book I develop and apply a methodology for agile security operations that is primarily focused on the process, rather than the structure, of a security operational capability. I discuss how these processes interact with each other using a map of the incident response process. The word agile is used because security operations need agility – the capability to quickly predict and adapt to a rapidly changing set of circumstances.

Agile has, in some contexts in the software development world, evolved into a complex and prescriptive framework for how to develop software. That is not how I operate here. Agile security operations are most certainly not a security or operations variety of agile or scrum, which are primarily software development methods. In the context employed here, agile security operations really focus on the tactical aspects of how teams *do* security, and how they embed, as a team, into a wider organization.

This book does not specifically adhere to one method of agile that is used in software development, nor does it get overly prescriptive in the practices and methods, although there is enough information here to do so if you want. Security operations, and how they are best done, are specific to each business and need to be carefully tailored and designed to meet the needs of that business. It is important that you adopt a framework that incorporates the idiosyncrasies and context of your business and implement what works for you.

This book will not focus in detail on the latest technology, gadgetry, tools, or clever attack approaches that are common to cybersecurity. In fact, in this book, I care little about such things at all (although they are interesting). This book instead focuses on tactics: the ethos and the way of thinking you need to successfully thwart cyber adversaries in your organization, as well as the processes that drive a credible security capability.

I run my teams, and wrote this book, from the viewpoint that what matters most in security teams is their grasp of context, key concepts, systems, and operations, and the many ways in which they influence the business. To the extent that this book hands down *tools*, those are the ones that matter most. In security, as elsewhere now, technical tools and approaches are subject to constant and rapid change. The grasp of the technical intricacies of tools is a threshold variable: teams need enough proficiency with the tools to be effective, but beyond that point, it is what they do with them that matters in how much they can influence and improve the security posture of the business.

Despite decades of hawking strategy and best practice by consultants, security has not markedly improved in many businesses, and from the viewpoint of the executive, matters have probably gotten worse.

Companies the world over are now making significant investments in security. Yet the ongoing drumbeat of cyber-breaches suggests that these investments matter less than should be the case. This situation needs to change. It can, if we improve our processes, work on embedding security teams into the organization, and develop the right ethos in our security teams.

Who this book is for

The intended audience for this book is security leadership, especially people managing security operation centers, security engineers, and security analysts. CISO, CDO, and CIO-level decision-makers will also benefit from this book. Some intermediate-level knowledge of incident response, cybersecurity, and threat intelligence is necessary to get started with the book.

What this book covers

Chapter 1, How Security Operations Are Changing, discusses how the landscape of security operations is changing and the pressures that are forcing that change. I focus on why security is hard and why the traditional measures in use in IT are failing when it comes to security.

Chapter 2, Incident Response – A Key Capability in Security Operations, focuses on the aim and purpose of incident response, and the reasons why incident response is the key security capability.

Chapter 3, Engineering for Incident Response, discusses the engineering aspects of incident response, from the viewpoint that incident response is a continuing operational activity that defines agile security operations. We will primarily build on the incident response loop to develop an agile framework for security operations and discuss some of the engineering aspects. This will be the final chapter that builds the framework for agile security operations, and the focus will be both on the agile security operations process and how tooling needs change as a result of that process.

Chapter 4, Key Concepts in Cyber Defense, discusses some key concepts of resilience that need to be understood for the rest of the book. This chapter will introduce the key concepts that make up the culture and ethos of agile security: chaos, constraints, defensibility, strategy, and tactics, and will focus on how to apply them correctly, as well as presenting further pointers to more detailed resources easily available on the internet. This chapter will use the earlier concept of the Cynefin framework to delve deeper into these concepts and how they shape thinking during incident response.

Chapter 5, Defensible Architecture, focuses on the development of defensible architecture. The main idea of defensible architecture is that it focuses on incident response in an environment during the design stage and tries to maximize the options available to defenders.

Chapter 6, Active Defense, takes the lessons from the previous chapter to heart and integrates them into a credible defense, taking us from response activities to tactics to strategy. This chapter focuses on the tactic of active defense and how it is implemented. Active defense is the practice of intelligence-driven breach detection, containment, and purposed engineering that is capable of dealing with persistent and advanced attackers.

Chapter 7, How Secure Are You? – Measuring Security Posture, tackles the difficult problem of measuring security posture and especially measuring and communicating the value that security operations bring to the organization. Traditionally, these discussions have focused on the reduction of risk, rather than driving business value. This chapter focuses on how practitioners should have these discussions in the context of business value and strategy.

Chapter 8, Red, Blue, and Purple Teaming, covers how active defense applies the principles of blue teaming. A purple team adds a certain amount of adversity to a blue team. Purple teaming aims to give a direct answer to the question, *Are we vulnerable?*, in ways that can be directly communicated to the business. This chapter outlines how organizations can get the most out of threat hunting and purple teaming.

Chapter 9, Running and Operating Security Services, explains how security operations done well revolve around six different security services. This chapter expands on security operations to the complete set of services that need to be run in the context of a security program with incident response at its core. Defining precise services in the context of a business environment is very important: it allows service strategies to be developed for these services, and allows monitoring and evaluation of these services, just like any other IT service. Many organizations struggle with cyber security precisely because they do not quite understand what the essential cyber security services are and the value they deliver to the business.

Chapter 10, Implementing Agile Threat Intelligence, covers the fact that threat intelligence requires a significant amount of organizational readiness. A credible threat intelligence program consists of a number of activities that are best performed in the context of agile security operations, such as curation, threat hunting and tasking, as well as adversary simulation.

To get the most out of this book

This book focuses primarily on methods and concepts and does not require a technical setup.

Download the color images

We also provide a PDF file that has color images of the screenshots/diagrams used in this book. You can download it here: `https://static.packt-cdn.com/downloads/9781801815512_ColorImages.pdf`.

Conventions used

There are a number of text conventions used throughout this book.

Bold: Indicates a new term, an important word, or words that you see onscreen. For example, words in menus or dialog boxes appear in the text like this. Here is an example: "This chapter will draw together many of the strands from previous chapters and develop an approach to the core of security operations called **active defense**."

> **Tips or Important Notes**
> Appear like this.

Get in touch

Feedback from our readers is always welcome.

General feedback: If you have questions about any aspect of this book, mention the book title in the subject of your message and email us at customercare@packtpub.com.

Errata: Although we have taken every care to ensure the accuracy of our content, mistakes do happen. If you have found a mistake in this book, we would be grateful if you would report this to us. Please visit www.packtpub.com/support/errata, selecting your book, clicking on the Errata Submission Form link, and entering the details.

Piracy: If you come across any illegal copies of our works in any form on the Internet, we would be grateful if you would provide us with the location address or website name. Please contact us at copyright@packt.com with a link to the material.

If you are interested in becoming an author: If there is a topic that you have expertise in and you are interested in either writing or contributing to a book, please visit authors.packtpub.com.

Share Your Thoughts

Once you've read *Agile Security Operations*, we'd love to hear your thoughts! Scan the QR code below to go straight to the Amazon review page for this book and share your feedback.

https://packt.link/r/1801815518

Your review is important to us and the tech community and will help us make sure we're delivering excellent quality content.

Section 1: Incidence Response: The Heart of Security

Part 1 establishes incident response as the "why" of security. That incident response is the heart of security should be clear on a moment's reflection: without cybersecurity incidents, there would be no need to have a security team. Yet the model in which incident response sits at the core of security efforts is not widely used. This part of the book explores agile security from this viewpoint.

This part of the book comprises the following chapters:

- *Chapter 1, How Security Operations Are Changing*
- *Chapter 2, Incident Response – A Key Capability in Security Operations*
- *Chapter 3, Engineering for Incident Response*

1
How Security Operations Are Changing

Cybersecurity is increasingly important for many organizations. It manifests itself as business risk. Security operations are a key security capability that organizations must implement to be effective in deterring and resolving the effects of cyber-attacks and minimize cybersecurity risk to their business. However, the role and mechanics of security operations is often misunderstood. That is why you are reading this book.

This book is written from a viewpoint on cybersecurity that, for some, turns matters on its head . I take the view that cybersecurity operations, when done well, drive security leadership, auditing, reporting, and risk reduction. This is not the common view on how organizations implement cybersecurity operations. The usual approach, sketched very briefly, is that organizations need executive commitment, funding, a cybersecurity program, often driven by audit results, and a raft of security policies and risk heat maps to be effective. Their job is then to drive this down into the business. The measurement of this is then done with maturity models and metrics.

This book will overturn that view. The viewpoint that I will develop and work out in this book is the following:

- *Passing audits* is the result of security operations done well. Audits do not drive improvement – making improvements in security operations drives improvement overall.

- Security operations vitally *develop and enrich* cybersecurity conversations at executive level mainly through the enhanced visibility they provide. Having a conversation about what happens on your network as opposed to what one reads about in the newspaper is inherently more powerful and convincing, especially if it can be backed up with evidence.

- The visibility and context provided by well-executed cybersecurity operations inherently changes the *strategy and risk* discussion, leading to better grounded risk and compliance programs.

- Building in the visibility and response components into applications and networks from the outset leads to better *security architecture* and changes the conversation from security being a blocker to security being an enabler of the business.

- If security operations are the core of an organization's cyber risk management, then the activities undertaken to resolve security *incidents* are at the heart of security operations. The viewpoint that I will take in this book, and that in my view defines agile security operations, is that effective incident response is the key measure when it comes to risk reduction from threats. In turn, the need to perform incident response then drives the rest of the security operations.

The *operations* piece of cybersecurity also needs funding, commitment, policies, and risk management. Doing cybersecurity operations well is not an excuse to get rid of these things. The difference is a radically changed conversation about their impact and use. Cybersecurity operations, done well, provide a vital context and enrichment to the executive and business conversation that will lead to a tight integration between cybersecurity and the business, reduce risk more effectively, and, in short, lead to an organization that is defensible from a tooling (technical), cultural (people), and management (process) perspective. The part between brackets is sometimes referred to as the **people, process, and technology (PPT)** framework.

The focus of this chapter is on the following:

- Understanding the role of security operations in risk management

- Defining security operations

- Understanding why security operations need to be agile

The chapter is structured as follows:

- Why security is hard
- Security incidents
- Security solutions in search of a problem
- The scope of security operations
- Where security operations turn agile

Why security is hard

In many organizations, implementing security is hard work. At a technical level, security is often seen as a blocker, at a tactical level, security considerations may change how the business operates, and at a strategic and political level, security often raises problems that many organizations prefer to ignore. This section will place security operations at the core of a security program and introduce the five types of cyber defense.

Security operations

This book takes the view that security operations are the heart of a security program. When organizations do their security operations well, they generate the necessary context to develop strategy, policies, and reporting, and gain the most benefit from audits.

The centrality of security operations is a somewhat unpopular view: much of what we see in security writing, focuses heavily on technology – which is the implementation side of security – or strategy, which focuses on the management and maturity of the program. By not considering security operations, the focus of too many organizations is still on prevention and controls. While prevention and controls are important, in this book I argue – based on experience – that they are the result of good security operations rather than the cause.

In a nutshell, security operations are an organization's capability to detect and respond to adversarial events on their systems and networks.

That is a mouthful, but we can unpack this a bit. *Detection* speaks to the capability of an organization to notice that something is wrong on their networks, preferably in an early stage of an attack, *respond* speaks to their capability to deal with such an event. *Adversarial* indicates that the event is caused by humans and has a specific component of intent.

In this book, I'll focus specifically on security operations and the ethos needed to create and sustain a security team that excels in security operations.

Therefore, I'll stay away from talking too much about either technology and strategy and instead focus heavily on tactics. **Tactics** – the specialty of security operations – is the nitty-gritty of how organizations respond to actual attacks, threats, vulnerabilities, and adversarial activity on their systems and networks.

If you think of strategy as the *why* of security, and the technology as the *what*, then tactics is the *how* – how do we realistically implement a risk program, how do we use that technology that has just been bought, and how do we secure an enterprise? These are the questions I will aim to answer in this book, and it is a critical connecting layer between technology and strategy that has not received the attention it deserves.

Cybersecurity, threats, and risk

Cybersecurity is traditionally approached from the viewpoint of business risk management. This creates a disconnect with security operations, and that fundamental disconnect makes security in many organizations harder than it needs to be.

To understand this better, we can look at how risk management usually approaches areas of risk. While the view of risk management I develop here is very simplified, it captures all the essentials. Risk management is typically based on a risk register, where risks are enumerated and given a priority of *high*, *medium*, or *low* (or a color-coded scale) based on both the exposure to the risk (the likelihood) and the impact (the consequence). In most cases, these assessments are subjective and dependent on the sector and context.

Risk management then relies on a matrix of controls to manage risk. Broadly speaking, risk treatment has four options: prevention, reduction, acceptance, or transfer. Prevention means that the organizations put in a device or measure that prevents the risk from materializing. Reduction means that some compensating control is developed that controls the risk, or at least make it visible in time.

Acceptance of risk means just that – the risk is accepted by the organization and no further action is undertaken to address it; consequences will have to be dealt with as they occur. This can happen, for instance, when a risk is too costly or cumbersome to address, or when the costs and effort associated with addressing it make no sense from the viewpoint of the risk accepted.

A transfer of risk occurs when the risks are borne by a third party, for instance in the case when an organization buys cyber insurance. We will have more to say on cyber insurance in *Chapter 7, How Secure Are You? – Measuring Security Posture*

Once this table is complete, risks are then prioritized, mitigations costed and budgeted, and the budgets for the highest risks are approved. Then it's rinse and repeat.

> **Measuring cybersecurity risk**
>
> While you might think that risk management is a typical *business* way of dealing with the risks posed by cybersecurity and is therefore easily understood by senior leaders in an organization, you would be wrong. In *How to Measure Anything in Cybersecurity Risk, Wiley, 2016*, Douglas Hubbard and Richard Seiersen argue passionately and in depth that this method of dealing with risk is a failure and does not work. While cybersecurity is indeed a business risk, we need to come up with a better method to communicate and treat risk.
>
> In *Chapter 7, How Secure Are You? – Measuring Security Posture*, we will return to the topic of how to make *security* relevant in a business context based on the model of security operations.

Security operations do not work this way. Security operations focus primarily on dealing with issues as they occur – that is, they focus on the here and now. Beyond the here and now, they focus on threats in the context of the business, and devise methods of detecting those threats.

To better understand the depth of the chasm that opens in this way, it helps to have a clear understanding of how organizations deal with cyber risk. Dealing with cyber risk from the perspective of a risk management framework leads an organization to put in passive defenses: things such as firewalls, antivirus, network controls, and access lists to form a defense in depth architecture. At worst, a strong focus on traditional risk can cause misspending on *silver bullets*: expensive security solutions that generally do much less than they promise, sometimes because the environment is not mature enough to make the most of the investment. Except for the silver bullet, passive defenses are all necessary in credible cyber defense, but they overlook large areas that organizations should also address when considering cyber defense.

Figure 1.1 shows a risk treatment approach to threats that is often used in cybersecurity. Where a threat is identified, it is usually translated into risk, and then the risk treatment process defines whether a vulnerability exists and what the extent of it is (sometimes called the **attack surface**). Several controls look at how to reduce exposure, how to mitigate it (for example, by timely patching), and arrive at a residual risk that can be put on the heat map, or further reduced:

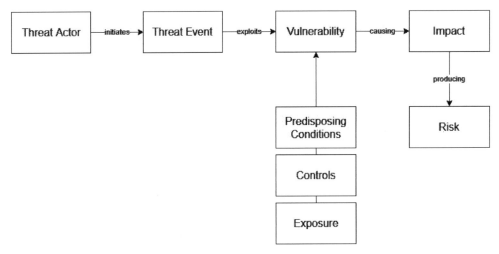

Figure 1.1 – Risk treatment of threats

This approach to threats focuses on passive defense. Thereby it misses out on important additional components of cybersecurity defense. Specifically, it misses out on what organizations may do (and, in my view, should do) in the areas of architecture, passive defense, active defense, intelligence, and perhaps even offense. These together make up the five types of cyber defense, which we discuss next.

Five types of cyber defense

As Rob Lee points out in *The Sliding Scale of Cyber Security* (2015) (`https://www.sans.org/reading-room/whitepapers/ActiveDefense/sliding-scale-cyber-security-36240`), passive defense is only one of the five available modes of defense that organizations should consider when designing a cyber risk program. The five options sit on a spectrum, ranging from architecture, through passive defense to active defense, intelligence, and offense.

This spectrum can be read as follows:

- **Architecture** focuses on the design of systems so that they are as secure as possible. As part of architecture, we consider possible threats to the system and how the system can be made resilient against those threats. One of the most important aspects of architecture is threat modeling. We will discuss architecture in *Chapter 5, Defensible Architecture*.

- **Passive defense** focuses on the defense in depth and control framework that implements several systems (such as firewalls). These systems are added as preventive capabilities to the architecture to ensure that the system is robust against common attacks without constant human intervention. Packet Filters, for instance, allow traffic on ports and/or protocols only and will drop any packet that does not conform to its rules without human intervention.

- **Active defense** focuses specifically on threats and their contexts as they manifest themselves to us as defenders and is one of the key activities of agile security operations. Active defenders pick up what passive defenses miss. Active defense builds and maintains context and focus on active threats, based on a superior understanding of the environment. We will return to active defense in *Chapter 6, Active Defense*.

- **Intelligence** is the knowledge that an organization has about the tactics, techniques, and procedures of its adversaries. We will return to intelligence in *Chapter 10, Implementing Agile Threat Intelligence*.

- **Offense** focuses on the *legal* actions that a defender can take to disrupt or degrade an attacker's infrastructure. This may, for instance, include *takedown* actions where an attacker's infrastructure is removed from the internet by an authorized body.

Figure 1.2 gives a representation of the five defense modes and the respective focus of risk-driven and operations-driven security programs. Well-managed operationally driven programs will tend to expand to encompass the five modes of defense, whereas risk-driven programs will tend to focus on architecture and passive defense:

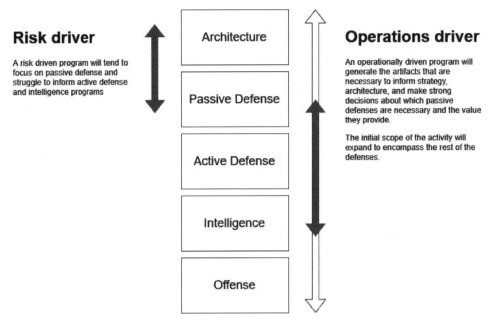

Figure 1.2 – A representation of the five defense modes and the respective focus of risk-driven and operations-driven security programs

Risk management and security operations therefore operate from radically differing but also complementing perspectives and assumptions about how to best secure an organization.

This book is written from the conviction that starting with security operations, security risk management can be done much better than is usually the case. An operationally driven program changes the conversation from *driving down* an externally defined program to a fact-based discussion on what *happens* in this business.

It is, from that perspective, surprising that many organizations that do have extensive security programs and policy frameworks are weak when it comes to security operations.

> **The security 1%**
>
> In an interesting blog post (`https://taosecurity.blogspot.com/2020/10/security-and-one-percent-thought.html`), Richard Bejtlich points out that the people having *somewhat* credible detection and response capability form part of the security 1%. He focuses on membership in `first.org` and then performs a quick estimate of the percentage of organizations that would be able to mount a credible defense when they are attacked. The conclusion is that only around 1% of organizations would have detection and response capabilities and are not running *just planning and resistance/prevention functions*. While this is a back-of-the-envelope calculation, it does underscore the need to improve security operations across the board. The problem of the security 1% also leads to several other problems, especially the question of whether advanced penetration testing tools and IOCs should be made as widely available as they are: they are nearly useless to the security 99% but may lead to improvements in the capability of attackers, making the overall security situation worse.

The focus on security operations does not mean that governance, risk, and compliance are unimportant. The main takeaway from this section is that the focus on security operations as a central activity alters the point where organizations should start *first*: governance, risk, and compliance is not a strong starting point for a security program in the initial stage – it is better to focus on developing operations that inform the governance program, and develop the governance, risk, and compliance program from what the security operations discover.

All the preceding points hinge on the assumption that an operations-driven security program is managed well. In *Chapter 7, How Secure Are You? – Measuring Security Posture*, we will return to the topic of governance, risk, and compliance in detail, and outline how a well-managed program can base itself on its operations.

Security incidents

A security incident is what most organizations hope will never happen. In agile security operations, incidents are the lifeblood of defense. During incidents, attackers reveal important information about their capabilities, intentions, methods, and tools, thereby turning a *threat* into reality. Good defenders will take advantage of the opportunity they are offered in this way to learn more about threats and improve their operations once the incident is over.

But to do this effectively, we need to be crystal clear about the intent and mode of incident response that organizations need to deploy. Learning from an attack is not useful if an organization doesn't survive the attack.

Cyber incident response has four key aims:

- Minimize attacker dwell time to the point where attackers are incapable of achieving their objectives

- Limit lateral movement of attackers on the network (for example, through defensible architecture)

- Prevent re-entry into the network after closure of an incident (evict successfully)

- Understand attackers' motivation and capability

The first aim of cyber defense is to ensure that an attacker – any attacker – will not achieve their objective and will be forced to leave before they achieve what they came for. This is quite an important point to understand: contrary to common opinion, the aim of cyber defense is not to prevent any attack at all costs, it is to prevent the adverse consequences resulting from an attack. Smart or experienced (or both) defenders know that attacks cannot be prevented, but they can only be dealt with once they occur.

Dwell time – the time attackers get to spend on our networks before they are discovered – is usually measured in months for the most advanced attacks. This really means that defense teams must improve their visibility and opportunities to detect the presence of attackers.

The second aim is to limit lateral movement of attackers or *slow them down*. The first point of compromise is rarely the end goal of an attacker, and attackers will need to *pivot* – or move laterally – to the point where they want to be. A hardened architecture with identity, data, and network segmentation will make it harder for attackers to do so and provide more opportunities to discover an attacker before they do their damage.

The third aim is to evict successfully and prevent re-entry. This speaks to how the activities should be sequenced: if an attacker entered the network through a particular vulnerability or backdoor, make sure that this issue is fixed before an attacker is removed. Also, many attackers set up a series of re-entry points and backdoors, so sometimes it is better to observe an attacker for a while to determine what they are and then evict them once all backdoors are discovered and can be closed.

The last aim is to discover as much as possible about an attacker while all this is going on. Also, store this information alongside any artifacts, somewhere securely. With many attacks going on, it is easy to forget important details and it is sometimes handy to have them at hand once the same attacker comes knocking again.

> **The Q model**
>
> Thomas Rid and Ben Buchanan developed a model for the attribution of cyber incidents that also indicates some of the key problems with incident response (*Journal of Strategic Studies, Vol. 38, 2015, pp. 4-37,* `https://www.tandfonline.com/doi/abs/10.1080/01402390.2014.977382`; a copy is also available on the author's personal website `https://ridt.co/d/rid-buchanan-attributing-cyber-attacks.pdf`).
>
> The Q model is primarily intended to address the complexity in attributing cyber-attacks, but also contains much that is useful during and after incident response.
>
> The idea is that attribution, like incident response, takes place on a strategic, operational, and tactical/technical layer, and focuses on the concept, the practice, and the communication/reporting.
>
> A detailed diagram of the Q model can be found in the supplemental material on the publisher's website: `https://ndownloader.figstatic.com/files/1860725`.

Security solutions in search of a problem

Before we really go into the nitty-gritty of security operations, I need to make one more point. A trivial one. Technological silver bullets don't exist. The security field is rife with solutions that pretend to be able to solve most of an organization's security problems (that is, address its risk) in a single stroke of technology (it should come as no surprise that this never works).

Organizations that fall for the seductive sales pitches of the silver bullets are getting less protection from their security investments than they think they are, misunderstand their real risks, and are likely to underinvest in security capability. A large reason for the failure of advanced tooling in immature businesses is that advanced tooling is seen as a silver bullet, is not understood in context, and lacks much of the data it needs to be effective. Even if the solutions themselves work as advertised, the implementation may fail primarily due to three reasons:

- They fail to understand and appreciate the context in which these security solutions work and fail to consider whether the right conditions for these solutions are in place.

- They fail to consider whether they can feed these solutions with the right data at the right time.

- They do not consider the impact on operations. Sometimes security technology needs a lot of fine-tuning by people who understand the context and do not work *out of the box.*

Robust security operations play a significant role in avoiding such a misspend, since it is only through security operations that organizations can understand the context in which advanced tooling functions best, the value it can provide, and the data and visibility it needs to be effective.

The scope of security operations

It is a mistake to think that the scope of security operations is limited to information technology, or wherever there is a computer or network. This is a leftover of a time when security operations were centered around network intrusion detection and malware operations.

These days, common exploits such as business email compromise are very common and successful. Business email compromise does not involve a technical intrusion on the network but instead exploits a business process. It involves sending an email to a person in an organization, pretending to be someone else, and then asking for money to be transferred for some reason.

The focus of this book will be how to do security operations well. Security operations done well focus as heavily on the context of security as they do on the technology. This means understanding the business and its operations as well as security technology.

What security operations do differently is that they view people, processes, and technology with an adversarial mindset: the view of an attacker.

Where security operations turn agile

Up to this point, we have discussed why security operations are central to a credible defense capability and a credible cyber program. But why do security operations need to be agile?

Agile is primarily a software methodology that just happens to describe, in my view, how the best security teams have already been operating for a while.

We can understand this better by considering the agile manifesto (`https://agilemanifesto.org/`) and recasting it in the context of security operations. The agile manifesto has four tenets:

- Individuals and interactions over processes and tools
- Working software over comprehensive documentation
- Customer collaboration over contract negotiation
- Responding to change over following a plan

We have stressed multiple times that security operations focus on context, adversity of events, and use processes as tools. In this sense, security operations as we will develop them in this book are agile – they put individuals and interactions first.

Agile incident response

During incidents, it may be necessary to develop methods that work in the detection and deterrence of a specific attacker. During incidents, there is often no time to develop extensive documentation – although things do need to be written down and communicated. How security teams communicate during incidents is often like how agile software development teams communicate – regular standups, rapid interaction, and teamwork in dealing with a volatile situation.

Collaboration with the business and external parties may be crucial during the response phase of an incident. It is often advisable to have the right agreements in place with key partners before an incident, but an incident is not the time to consider extensive agreements and negotiations.

It is important that security teams share aggressively. There are several protocols that are widely accepted and used for sharing incident and attack data with outside parties.

The most common one, mostly used in enterprise security operations outside the intelligence community, is the **traffic light protocol** (`https://www.first.org/tlp/`). The traffic light protocol has, as you would expect, the colors red, amber, and green as well as white. The definitions of the colors are given in the web page. In practice, the meanings of the colors are as follows (although they sometimes change):

- **TLP: Red**: May not be shared with anyone outside the current conversation without the explicit permission of the person who shared the data. This permission must be asked for and given.

- **TLP: Amber**: May be shared on a *need-to-know* basis with members of the participants' organizations.

- **TLP: Green**: May be shared on a *need-to-know* basis within the community.

- **TLP: White**: Public disclosure subject to copyright.

Incident handling is primarily a process of anticipating change, responding to change, and having the ability to counter attackers' moves. In this sense, incident response and security operations differ in an important respect from software development: in software development, there is no party *on the other side* that actively tries to counter our moves and stay invisible, and who means us harm.

Security incident response often takes place under conditions of volatility, uncertainty, complexity, and ambiguity, summarized by the acronym VUCA. Agile stresses transparency and open communications, as well as accountability in its processes. This makes it suitable for dealing with incident response situations as well. The details of how that happens will be discussed in *Chapter 2, Incident Response – A Key Capability in Security Operations*.

Agile security operations

There are also good reasons for security operations to adopt an agile framework outside of the immediacy of incident response. Many of them will become clear later in this book. In this section, I will contrast *agile,* or *capability*, which I prefer, with the more common approach of using maturity models to guide security development.

Maturity models tend to focus on processes and tools and classify operations in categories such as *ad hoc, basic, managed,* and *optimized*. The problem is that the focus is on processes and tools, rather than people and capability. This is the wrong focus for security. Teams should focus on capability rather than maturity for the following reasons.

Security, both attack and defense, moves faster than other technology areas. This is particularly the case during incident response, but even with this pressure removed, developments in security are very rapid. A maturity model will have trouble dealing with the rapid evolution, since it is the model itself that must change to account for change, not the team or the practices.

Traditional risk management frameworks, which maturity models evolved from, are a poor fit for cybersecurity. This not only means that the traditional risk management methods have a propensity to lead us to the wrong solution, but also to the wrong sort of security operations. We have already seen that traditional risk models tend to leave out critical components of cyber defense; this is also true at a team and operations level. Maturity models focus on processes and repeatable playbooks and treat a security operations team as they treat a helpdesk. Many security operations teams have a *Tier 1, Tier 2*, and *Tier 3* approach to security that is a poor measure of true capability and may require hand-off documentation in a time of crisis as an incident moves through its levels.

Incidents provide a rapid feedback, learning, and adaptation environment in which capability trumps maturity all the time.

Many small to mid-size organizations have a need to develop and deploy a credible cyber defense capability. A strong focus on maturity leaves out the necessary focus on what is necessary for them, and instead leads them to think that developing a credible cyber defense capability is an impossible task. It is not.

Lastly, there is the human factor. Maturity models lead us to a focus on processes, documentation, and repeatability. Security already has a workforce problem. The prospect of becoming a cog in a wheel will not be very attractive to the people who can have the most impact in this field.

Summary

In this chapter, we have introduced several concepts and reasons why security operations are central to a security program and inform and enhance both the strategy and risk management of a cybersecurity program by providing real facts on threats, context, effectiveness of controls, and effective policies.

Security operations, moreover, have a natural tendency toward agility, and many aspects of the agile methodology also apply in security teams. Even stronger, it could be argued that the best security teams have already worked in an agile way before the term became popular.

This book will not advocate dropping all regimentation, reporting, and discipline from security operations. It will argue that there is a better way. Security operations do need strong discipline and regimentation, and there is even room for processes and repeatability, but the stakes are too high to settle for suboptimal.

In the next chapter, we will focus more extensively on incident response as a core practice of agile security operations.

2
Incident Response – A Key Capability in Security Operations

It is quite common during incident response to find that the indicators of an attack were there long before an incident was declared. It is also a fact that the *dwell time* of attackers in a victim environment can be in the order of months. Organizations are attempting to keep attackers out, but they don't seem to be succeeding.

In this chapter, I will argue that this is because organizations are not adapting to an *assumption of compromise*. An assumption of compromise is the result of the realization that adversaries can stay undetected for a long time, and hence it is likely that at any point in time, a part of the network is compromised or under an attack that has not yet been detected. Even in cases where an assumed compromise philosophy is adopted, the necessary lessons are not always learned: assumed compromise involves developing a continuous and advanced process of incident response, where a *normal* state of no incident is becoming ever rarer.

The key lesson of an *assumed compromise* state is that organizations are also finding themselves in a state of continuous incident response. That is the key reason why incident response is the key capability of security operations.

In the previous chapter, we discussed the four key objectives of security operations:

- Minimize attacker dwell time to the point where attackers are incapable of achieving their objectives.
- Limit lateral movement of attackers in the network.
- Prevent re-entry into the network after the closure of an incident.
- Understand attacker motivation and capabilities.

The philosophy of assumed compromise takes these objectives to the rest of security operations.

This is not how organizations usually do incident response. The best practice recommendation is that incident response should follow the incident response cycle, a structured way to resolve large-scale breaches and incidents. In this chapter, I will extend the incident response cycle to illustrate how incident response practices can and must evolve to meet the conditions of assumed compromise.

Predictable and repeatable execution of the four capabilities that make up incident response is the key to robust and predictable security operations. Beyond this point, all other elements that make up security operations are in support of this goal.

In this chapter, we will discuss what an incident response capability based on an assumed compromise philosophy looks like.

Specifically, in this chapter we will focus on the following:

- The incident response cycle and the attack kill chain
- Why **agile** is a good model for incident response
- How to extend to incident response cycle to include agile security operations
- How to learn from incidents and drive continuous improvement

The chapter is structured in the following way:

- Facing up to breaches
- Knowing an incident – detection and analysis
- Branches and pivots – how incidents change
- Agile incident response
- Learning from incidents – from resolution to tactics to strategy

Facing up to breaches

Organizations should have a plan for dealing with security incidents. The **incident response cycle** is a structured template for developing and maintaining such a plan, and it is also a good place to start our discussion of agile security operations.

The incident response cycle, which will form an important aspect of agile security operations, is depicted in the following figure:

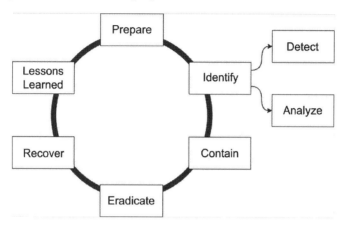

Figure 2.1 – The incident response cycle with the identification stage split into detection and analysis steps

The incident response cycle describes a process for handling incidents in several separate steps. Somewhat dependent on the organization, the incident response cycle can take several forms and may involve a somewhat different set of steps.

We will first discuss the background to the incident response cycle. In the following sections, we will briefly discuss the NIST incident response cycle and the SANS incident response cycle.

The incident response cycle

Incident handling follows the structured processes of the incident response cycle. Incident response cycles are particularly suited to dealing with large-scale, one-off incidents. Notable varieties of the incident response cycle have been developed by SANS and NIST.

The NIST incident response cycle

The **National Institute for Standards and Technology (NIST)** has published a 4-step incident response process that is like SANS, but has the containment, eradication, and recovery steps as a single step. The process is available as the NIST 800-61 standard. It is available here: `https://www.nist.gov/privacy-framework/nist-sp-800-61`.

The following diagram is a representation of the NIST cycle:

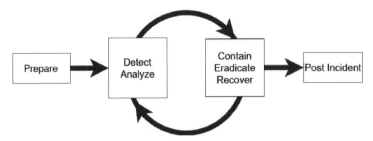

Figure 2.2 – The NIST incident response cycle

The NIST incident response cycle consists of the following steps:

- **Preparation**: The preparation stage involves getting ready to handle an incident, as well as taking the necessary steps to prevent attacks on the system from becoming successful.

- **Detection** and **analysis**: The SANS model for incident response recommends that organizations understand their attack vectors and develop playbooks for handling these types of incidents.

- **Containment**, **eradication**, and **recovery**: This set of activities focuses first on making sure that an incident does not overwhelm the capability of defenders through containment of the incident. Eradication and recovery focus on how organizations evict the attackers and recover their systems. In the SANS model, there is a mini cycle that flows back from this stage to the detection and analysis stage to indicate that during containment and eradication, further analysis and detection may be required. This stage also contains a focus on forensic data preservation.

- **Post-incident** activity: This step contains a review process that allows an organization to document an incident, do no-blame reviews, and document lessons that were learned. Incidents can also be evaluated using the metrics discussed in the following section.

The documentation of the NIST incident response cycle is comprehensive and contains a large amount of documented best practices in handling computer incidents.

An important feature of the NIST incident response cycle is the *inner loop* between the detect and analyze step and the contain, eradicate, and recover phase. The activities that teams perform in this inner loop will be discussed in more detail in *Chapter 6, Active Defense*.

Metrics for incident response

The NIST guide also develops a set of metrics to measure the effectiveness of the incident response process. In *Chapter 7, How Secure Are You? – Measuring Security Posture*, we will focus on the topic of security metrics.

The SANS incident response cycle

As a brief alternative, we'll look at the SANS incident response cycle. The SANS institute provides a large amount of information security research, training, and online resources to practitioners. The SANS incident response cycle forms part of their course on hacker techniques and training (SANS 504) and is available in the Incident Handlers Handbook: `https://www.sans.org/reading-room/whitepapers/incident/incident-handlers-handbook-33901`. There is a cheat sheet here: `https://www.sans.org/cyber-security-courses/hacker-techniques-exploits-incident-handling/`.

The SANS incident response cycle consists of six steps:

- **Preparation**: In the preparation stage, organizations ensure that they have an incident response plan and the necessary policies, develop the team structure for incident response, and define the triage system for security incidents, as well as the processes for each category of incident. This stage also includes the introduction of tooling and training.

- **Identification**: In the identification phase, an incident is identified and triaged, and the processes defined in the previous step are started.

- **Containment**: In the containment phase, defenders ensure that an attacker cannot do more damage by isolating the incident in the affected systems and preventing further spread.

- **Eradication**: This stage focuses on the removal of the attacker from the network by removing malicious artifacts, rebuilding systems where this is necessary, and ensuring that the access routes of the attacker into the infrastructure are blocked.

- **Recovery**: This stage focuses on the activities that will bring the organization back to its pre-incident state.

- **Lessons learned**: The focus here is on what the organization can do to prevent a reoccurrence of the attack, points of improvement in the process of handling incidents, and documenting the incident for future reference.

The SANS process maps closely to the NIST process, and organizations can equally well use either of the two. In some cases, requirements may be determined by compliance regimes or the cyber insurer.

How to use the incident response cycle

At each stage of the incident response cycle, a security team must have developed and deployed a set of practices that will allow it to function at its best. As an example, in the preparation stage, it is important that a team defines and documents the policies that will allow it to operate during an incident – the systems they will have to access to allow them to collect data on an incident, under what conditions the team can get that access, any necessary change controls, business owners, and the monitoring that is already in place.

Similarly, for the collection of data, a team should know what tooling to use and how to use that tooling. If necessary, prepare a jump bag.

The value of the incident response cycle to the business is that it allows you to think through an incident in advance, define what is required, and then ensure that the necessary components are developed, implemented, and maintained. It also assists with planning the phases and ensuring that organizations do not move to remediation too quickly, destroying evidence and information about the attack in the process.

Knowing an incident – detection and analysis

In this section, I will work primarily from the SANS incident response process but will divide the *identification* step into two separate steps – detection and analysis. This is because detection and analysis are two different engineering activities that are better separated once we center incident response as the core security practice and assume a state of perpetual compromise.

In a state of assumed compromise, it is vital that you know when to call an incident and how to analyze and respond to it. Detection and analysis are the two key activities:

- **Detection** focuses on how security teams detect that an incident may be occurring.

- **Analysis** focuses on whether an incident is occurring and what the severity of it is.

Detection engineering

Detecting incidents can happen in several ways. As an example, teams may monitor logs, antivirus, and network events, and the combination of these events determines that a security event is occurring. A **Security Information and Event Management** (**SIEM**) system may be used to automate collecting events from different sources and collate them to determine if an event has occurred through a detection engine.

> **SIEM**
>
> The definition of the SIEM in the Gartner IT Glossary reads, in part, "*SIEM technology aggregates event data produced by security devices, network infrastructure, systems and applications. The primary data source is log data, but SIEM technology can also process other forms of data, such as network telemetry. Event data is combined with contextual information about users, assets, threats and vulnerabilities.*"
>
> ```
> https://www.gartner.com/en/information-technology/
> glossary/security-information-event-management
> ```

A SIEM will generally use correlation rules to determine whether an incident has occurred, and the quality and review of such correlation rules is a key determinant of the value of the SIEM to organizations.

Detection engineering takes this a step further and deploys detections as code, taking the context of the business into account.

The problem with many logging tools, standard SIEMs, and security tools is that they generate a firehose of data, events, and alerts that need to be triaged, analyzed, put in a ticketing system, and reported, leading to analyst burnout, and increasing the chances that important alerts are missed. The firehose of data has poor quality control.

It is worth spending a small amount of time considering what quality control of an alert stream is. The following table summarizes the possible outcomes of an alert system in a four-by-four matrix, determined by whether an alert was generated or not, and whether the alert was true or false.

False Positive
A security alert that does not represent a real event. There is nothing to see here, but time was spent to analyze it. Leads to analyst burnout and alert fatigue.

False Negative
A security event did occur but there is no security alert. This security event is undetected and poses a risk to the business. It represents the blind spot of the tool.

True Positive
A security alerts that represents a real event and should be investigated.

True Negative
There is no security alert and no security event, so nothing to see here.

Figure 2.3 – The four-by-four matrix of detection possibilities and consequences

Many teams generate a lot of data through their tools but struggle to make sense of it—they are overwhelmed by false positives and lack of context. Attackers take advantage of this situation by aiming to develop techniques that evade simple detection mechanisms.

Detection engineering focuses on remediating this problem. It consists of the following high-level activities:

- Develop and maintain custom code that merges known and observed security intrusions with business and data context to be able to detect attacks on the organization.

- Work with analysts and engineers from the security team to turn data from past investigations into actionable detections.

- Work with architects, process, and data owners to develop new opportunities for detection of malicious activity, such as process abuse or specific threats to infrastructure (this is discussed in more detail in *Chapter 5, Defensible Architecture*).

- Develop and categorize proactive and reactive controls.

- Quality monitoring of detections: focus on the number of false positives, false negatives, true positives, and true negatives. Generally, the purpose is to decrease the number of false positives and false negatives and increase the number of true positives.

- Reduce the number of low-level alerts to fewer high-fidelity ones.

Enterprise detection

Enterprise detection relies on the practice of detection engineering as a systematic discipline that follows a structured process to use the data generated by monitoring and logging systems. See `https://www.sans.org/reading-room/whitepapers/analyst/detecting-malicious-activity-large-enterprises-39795`.

The detection engineering process, which will be discussed in more detail at various places in this book, is depicted in *Figure 2.2*. The analysis that is performed by the analyst can be based on a past incident, potential threats to an existing business process, or a quality improvement in an existing detection (which is then versioned in the repository).

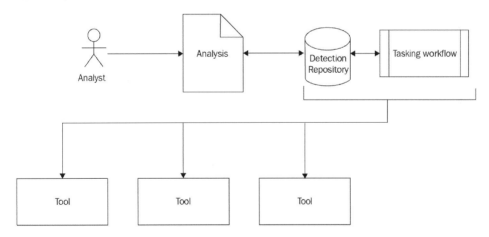

Figure 2.4 – The detection engineering process

Contributions to the detection engineering process can come from a variety of sources, such as the following:

- Subscriptions from commercial or open source feeds such as signatures and SIEM rulesets

- Previous or current incidents, especially if these have been captured in the form of **tactics, techniques, and procedures (TTPs)**

- External sources such as security news sites or blog posts with details of currently ongoing attacks

- Cyber threat intelligence sources (see *Chapter 10*, *Implementing Agile Threat Intelligence*)

Not all information about breaches needs to come from security infrastructure. Sometimes it is possible to re-purpose other logs in a security context.

Repurposing

Sometimes, already existing infrastructure tells you about breaches, even if it was not intended to do so. An example is, for instance, web server logs, which are sometimes used by developers to troubleshoot websites, but also contain a wealth of information that is useful in a security context. It is important that teams do not overlook the value that this data can bring.

Analyzing threats

After a threat is detected, it must be analyzed. Analysis, in the context of continuous compromise, uses forensic techniques to collect, collate, and contextualize data, and report on the findings.

Analysis consists of the following high-level activities:

- **Collection** of data is the process of using tools to collect the data that is necessary for the analysis from the affected system. Examples include memory collection, log file analysis, querying the system with tools such as `OSQuery` or `Velociraptor`, and disk imaging. Care must be taken that collection tools are forensically sound.

- **Collation** of data is combining the collected data into a single repository so that it can be searched and systematically analyzed. For log data, it is preferable to use a NoSQL platform, such as *Splunk* or *ELK*, to do this.

- **Contextualizing** refers to adding the necessary business and IT context to the data.

- **Reporting** is the process of capturing the findings. This does not need to be an official report, but it is important that teams capture the activities, assumptions, findings, and anything else worth noting down about an incident.

Analysis is not a linear process, but it may involve moving back from context to detection.

Branches and pivots – how incidents change

The incident response cycle is not necessarily linear. Even as we are handling an incident, the incident itself may change because the attacker moves from one system to another, or because the defenders discover additional areas of compromise related to the same attacker.

The evolution of cyber incidents is described in the *kill chain*, a model for how a cyber-attack develops.

The kill chain is a model for the evolution of a cyber-attack, not a prescriptive recipe for how an attacker should attack. Hence, attackers do not necessarily follow the kill chain. An especially important part of attacker movement is *lateral movement*, which is discussed toward the end of this section.

The kill chain model

The kill chain model was originally developed by Lockheed Martin to describe the development of a cyber-attack, especially by an advanced persistent threat actor using multi-stage attacks with targeted malware and remote-control components. The kill chain is a model for how cyber-attacks evolve; its purpose is to help defenders define and execute defensive actions at each stage of the chain.

> **Note**
>
> The term **Cyber kill chain**™ is trademarked by Lockheed Martin. In the following sections, we'll use the term *kill chain model* to denote the kill chain model in a computer security context to avoid the use of a narrowly defined trademarked term.

The kill chain model consists of seven steps:

1. In the **reconnaissance** phase, the attackers gather information on their victim's network, such as IP address ranges, exposed vulnerabilities, DNS names, websites, email servers, and anything else that can be used as an initial vector of compromise.

2. **Weaponization** is the development of the cyber-weapon that will be used in the attack. Weaponization has to involve development of both a delivery mechanism and a payload. For malware or phishing, it may also involve setting up external websites or command and control infrastructure that will be used during the attack.

3. **Delivery** is the delivery of the cyber-weapon to the victim, for instance via email or another mechanism.

4. **Exploitation** consists of achieving a form of code execution on the victim's system, or getting a victim to enter their details in a phishing page..

5. **Installation** covers the installing of the command-and-control and actions-on-objectives pieces of the malware.

6. **Command and control** focuses on remote control of the malware by the attacker, usually through some sort of communication channel.

7. **Actions on objectives** focuses on how the attacker achieves their objectives.

Development of the kill chain model

The kill chain model for cyber-attacks was originally developed by Hutchins, Cloppert, and Amin from Lockheed Martin (`https://www.lockheedmartin.com/content/dam/lockheed-martin/rms/documents/cyber/LM-White-Paper-Intel-Driven-Defense.pdf`). The purpose of the kill chain is to develop a model that decomposes the actions of adversaries during cyber incidents and then guides defenders to a set of defensive actions at each step of the chain. The aim of defense in the kill chain model is to ensure that attackers do not achieve their objectives.

The kill chain model has developed into several varieties, such as the universal kill chain (Pols) or the ICS kill chain developed by SANS. The universal kill chain model by Pols takes the effects of lateral movement into account and acts as a model of models that aggregates different kill chain models. The universal kill chain takes lateral movement into account by creating *loops* in the kill chain. A copy of the universal kill chain can be downloaded from here: `https://www.csacademy.nl/images/scripties/2018/Paul_Pols_-_The_Unified_Kill_Chain_1.pdf`.

The ICS kill chain focuses on an adaptation of the kill chain model. The ICS kill chain whitepaper can be downloaded from here: `https://www.sans.org/reading-room/whitepapers/ICS/industrial-control-system-cyber-kill-chain-36297`.

There has been a lot of discussion about the exact number of steps in the kill chain, or whether the kill chain model can be used in different types of attack. Ultimately, the aim of the kill chain model is to *guide defenders in how to thwart attackers*, and while extensive discussion about all the steps is possible, it is not very useful.

The kill chain model was developed to illustrate that defenders have several stages at which they can prevent an attacker from achieving their objectives, and to guide defensive actions for each stage in an attack.

The current trend is that the kill chain model is gradually replaced by the more comprehensive MITRE ATT&CK model, which is based on a model of **Tactics, Techniques, and Procedures (TTPs)**. The tactics in the ATT&CK model roughly match the stages in the kill chain model. This book is based more on the ATT&CK model than on the kill chain. The ATT&CK model will reappear at various stages in later chapters.

Expanding the options for defense

The understanding of cyber incidents is enriched by the kill chain. An awareness of the kill chain changes both the detection and analysis steps in incident response. As we have seen, the kill chain model was developed primarily to allow defenders to determine what defensive options are available to them once they understand the stage to which an attack has progressed. In terms of the incident response cycle, this means that a few things need to be considered in terms of the kill chain, especially detection, analysis, containment, and eradication:

- **Detection**: Coverage should include all aspects of the kill chain, rather than a single detection. Detection engineering needs to increase the chance that an attack can be picked up at any stage.

- **Analysis**: In addition to doing the forensic analysis of malicious artifacts, analysis also must consider the stage of the attack on the kill chain.

- One of the ways to determine the available options in the **containment** and **eradication** stage is to use one of the many Ds: Detect, Deny, Disrupt, Degrade, Deceive, and Destroy. The eradication stage effectively evicts the attacker from our network.

Considering attacks in the context of kill chain models, together with the variety of defensive options available, leaves a lot of room for defenders. Making the most of those options is the core of active defense, which we will discuss in more detail in *Chapter 6, Active Defense*.

Lateral movement

The initial point of compromise is rarely the objective of an attacker. Attackers do not necessarily adhere to the linear models for cyber-attacks that are suggested by the kill chain model. In many cases, attackers perform lateral movement in a victim's network, moving from an initial exploit to, for instance, reconnaissance of the infrastructure behind the firewall.

Lateral movement involves attackers moving from point to point in the network, often involving *living off the land*, or using the toolset that's already available on a compromised endpoint to move laterally. Lateral movement often involves tools such as *PowerShell*, Command Prompt, or other native administration tooling that is already present on the compromised infrastructure, and their usage is unlikely to trigger signature-driven detection systems.

One of the four objectives of incident response is to limit lateral movement on the network so that attackers will not be able to move between environments. Given that a large proportion of lateral movement involves living off the land, this involves managing permissions and accounts on the network. In *Chapter 3, Engineering for Incident Response*, we will discuss lateral movement in more detail.

For the purposes of this chapter, the existence and prevalence of lateral movement has important consequences:

- **Architecture**: *Defensible architecture* does not rely on hard outer shells, but instead uses, in addition to perimeter controls, detection and analysis capabilities deeper in the network.

- **Detection**: The techniques used in lateral movement widen the scope of what needs to be detected and need to be explicitly added to the detection framework. A problem is that the volume of traffic inside the network is usually larger than outside the network, meaning that significant capability needs to be deployed inside the network to build the necessary detections.

- **Analysis**: Living off the land techniques need to be recognized in the analysis step.

- **Response**: During incident response, an organization needs to slow the lateral movement of attackers. Conversely, the need to move laterally also slows attackers down and may give a (small and temporary) advantage to the defender.

Lateral movement is an important addition to the kill chain that adds new detection and analysis opportunities.

Agile incident response

In the previous chapter, we have argued that security operations are best done in an agile framework. This is even more true for incident response.

Even though cyber incident response is a technical capability, there are some non-technical considerations that are influential in how well organizations respond to and recover from incidents. These considerations also translate into aspects of agile security operations once we come to realize that the consequence of lateral movement is that multiple detection and analysis phases might be carried out to discover and analyze an event in its entirety.

Compromise is eternal

Once incident response becomes the key security capability and the core of security operations, incident response becomes not only a core process, but also a continuous process. The boundary between an *incident* and a *normal situation* dissolves, and the organization will manage multiple incidents in a continuous fashion. In this situation, an *assumed compromise* approach to cybersecurity becomes the norm.

> **A new philosophy for cybersecurity**
>
> The accounting firm PWC published a whitepaper entitled *Are you compromised but don't know it* in 2011, which outlines some of the key ideas of agile security operations, although they have evolved since then. Among others, this paper introduces the idea of the centrality of incident response because of assumed compromise. The original whitepaper has, to my knowledge, disappeared from the PWC website (although it is available through a search). A slide deck that outlines some of the key points may be found here: `https://www.imf-conference.org/ imf2014/docs/IMF2014-Assuming%20a%20state%20of%20 compromise.pdf`.

Many organizations do not define their security posture. By not doing so, they adopt an implicit default posture that somehow assumes that adversaries will never get in.

A posture of assumed compromise changes this assumption and with it changes the security conversation for the better. In this way, it helps security teams focus on the *business they are there to protect*.

The move from a default posture to assumed compromise quickly leads to a process of explication, clarifying the role of security to the business. This process introduces the somewhat confusing notion of *security posture*, which we will take up in more detail in *Chapter 7, How Secure Are You? – Measuring Security Posture*.

The question of acceptable security posture inherently revolves around business questions that cannot be outsourced to third parties, because the answers rely on a deep understanding of the business that outsourcers or consultants usually cannot provide.

To clarify the security posture, organizations must develop and consider the security context around the key business *processes* rather than *systems*. Three questions are useful to tease out what the business consequences of a security compromise look like:

- Which processes are key to the survivability of the business? What can we not do without?
- Which components in our system enable these processes?
- What is the business context to threats that the business currently faces in light of the answers to the previous two questions?

Good security leaders have ongoing conversations with the business around what is key now and into the future. Assumed compromise refocuses the security conversation from a fear-based *mission impossible* to a conversation about the *already available security capability*, as well as basic environment and system hygiene and visibility. This takes security from mission impossible to doable.

Incidents and compromises

It is useful to sharply distinguish between **incidents** and **compromise**.

An **incident** occurs when the business is down. Generally, in terms of the kill chain, having an incident means that the attackers have managed to achieve their objectives and the defenders have failed in their first objective: ensuring that attackers cannot achieve their objectives.

In comparison to incidents, a **compromise** is more benign. A compromise generally means that an attacker has managed to gain an initial foothold and is using tactics such as privilege escalation and discovery to try and escape that initial foothold, or move laterally. When we say compromise is eternal, what we are really advocating is eternal vigilance. The activities of attackers trying to escape their initial foothold can be detected and mitigated.

This is also the reason behind the second defender objective: to limit the lateral movement of attackers.

Why incident response needs to be agile

In the previous chapter, we discussed how security operations work better under an agile framework. This is even more so for incident response. Incident response gets the best results when it is approached in an iterative model that can quickly react to changes and anticipates the next step of the intruder in our systems and networks.

Figure 2.3 gives a high-level overview of how the incident response cycle—once lateral movement and iterations in detection, analysis, and containment are considered—maps to an agile framework. This figure is very similar to the inner loop in the NIST framework, with the exception that we are not considering the eradication and recovery part of the inner loop while the NIST framework, which has containment, eradication, and recovery as a single phase, does. This is debatable.

The incident declaration, the start of the process, leads to a series of iterative detect, analyze, and containment steps, which may, due to the lateral movement of an attacker, feed further detections, analysis, and containment.

As we will see in *Chapter 6, Active Defense,* the inner loop is in operation even in cases where no incident is declared. The main reason for this is that active defense is operative under conditions of incidents as well as compromises.

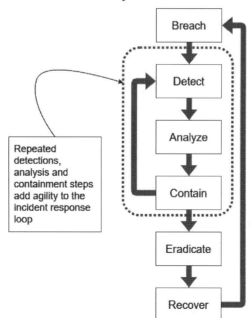

Figure 2.5 – Agile loops in the incident response process

Incident response does not immediately translate to agile, and the details of an agile incident response process will form the core of the next chapter.

Kanban or Scrum

As we will see in *Chapter 3, Engineering for Incident Response*, the agile methodology can be based on several underlying frameworks, the main ones being Kanban and Scrum. Scrum tends to be quite prescriptive, and any Scrum-based incident response framework would not be called Scrum but something else. The Kanban principles fit quite well with the process of incident response.

In the next chapter, *Chapter 3, Engineering for Incident Response*, we will develop a specific framework to manage and engineer for security incidents in an agile fashion.

Team structure for incident response

Incidents are confusing and volatile. This section introduces the key elements.

The team structure for incident response consists of three separate capabilities:

- **Operations** focuses on the activities of detection, analysis, forensics, and containment, and works together with planning to develop plans for eviction and recovery. Operations teams typically consist of members of the security team working alongside people from operations, development, and subject matter experts from the business.

- **Communication** focuses on both internal and external communication.

- **Planning** focuses on developing the plans and steps to best recover from an incident and considers the changes that are necessary to permanently evict attackers before systems are brought back online.

A diagram of the team structure is represented in the following figure:

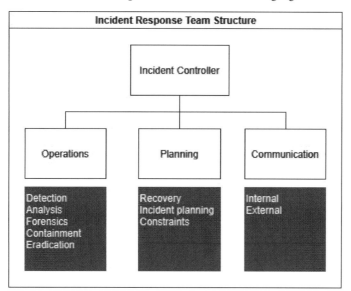

Figure 2.6 – Team structure for incident response teams

The operations team needs detection and forensics capability, while the planning team needs a robust understanding of the business context of an incident. In practice, the operations team is often constructed on the fly, whereas the communication and planning team can be determined beforehand.

Learning from incidents – from resolution to tactics to strategy

A final point we need to consider in this chapter is how organizations may learn from incidents.

Assuming an assumed compromise stance to cyber defense entails that current detected and resolved incidents are the best guide to the threats and risks facing the organization and what to do about them. This is in stark contrast to a model where a cyber defense strategy is prior to capability, and it represents a bottom-up model for strategy, one in which measurable defense activities take precedence over risk assessments and static defense.

The idea is that past incidents will be a guide to the likely future. Once the lessons of a past incident are identified, organizations must develop a strategy to ensure that the lesson is learned, and that tactics and operations change to align with the areas of known most likely threats.

There are, of course, dangers with this approach, the main one being that lack of visibility will lead to incidents going undetected and hence not being considered as a cyber risk to the organization. The *bottom-up strategy* approach should be accompanied by high-quality detection and analysis to mitigate this risk. What *high-quality* is in this context is determined by how well the visibility measures of an organization cover the kill chain of cyber-attacks.

Summary

In this chapter, we have laid the groundwork for understanding why incident response is the key security capability under an assumption of continuous compromise. We have adapted the incident response cycle to deal with conditions where security teams are responding to incidents in a continuous manner.

Specifically, this chapter has covered why a philosophy of assumed compromise requires changes to the incident response practice. In the assumed compromise model, incidents are constant and hence incident response becomes a continuous process.

We have discussed the kill chain model for cyber-attacks and argued that the reality of lateral movement implies that the kill chain model must be extended to include lateral movement. Moreover, the reality of lateral movement drives a preference for an agile incident response process.

We have also introduced a model for detection engineering, which we will return to in *Chapter 3, Engineering for Incident Response.*

We concluded this chapter with a discussion on how to drive a more effective security strategy from the bottom up by specifically developing the business context around our incident stream and translating this into a security posture. We will return to this topic in *Chapter 7, How Secure Are You? – Measuring Security Posture.*

In the next chapter, we will focus on engineering for incident response, specifically on how all the things we discussed in the previous chapters combine into an overall cyber defense.

3
Engineering for Incident Response

In the previous two chapters, we discussed security operations and incident response and looked at some of the key elements that come into play in incident response, such as the incident response cycle and the kill chain. We have also argued, albeit somewhat loosely, that *agile* is the best approach for both security operations and incident response. In this chapter, the aim is to tighten up that argument and develop an agile framework in more detail, as well as outline what relationships exist between existing agile approaches and agile security operations.

In this chapter, we will discuss the engineering aspects of incident response, from the viewpoint that *incident response is a continuing operational activity that defines agile security operations.*

We will primarily build on the incident response loop to develop an agile framework for security operations and discuss some of the engineering aspects. This will be the final chapter that builds the framework for agile security operations, and the focus will be both on the agile security operations *process* and how the *tooling needs* to change because of that process.

The key to understanding the agile extension of the incident loop is the realization that it is important, especially if we have assumed compromise, that the incident loop does not become a hamster wheel to nowhere, but instead facilitates the *improvement* of cyber defenses. The underlying idea is that actual *attacks* on your organization, once detected and handled properly, are the best guides to the *threats* faced by your organization, and hence also a robust guide to strategy. Threats, in turn, translate into risks, in a way we have discussed in *Chapter 1*, *How Security Operations Are Changing*. Hence, the data you gain from actual intrusions is too valuable to treat sloppily.

The agile method for security operations developed in this chapter, based as it is on specific engineering for incident response, focuses on how we can get the most out of an incident and use it to improve detection, analysis, containment, and eradication.

We will use the Mitre ATT&CK and Shield frameworks and integrate this understanding into an overall picture of defensible infrastructure and applications.

In this chapter, we will cover the following topics:

- From incident response to agile security operations engineering
- A brief discussion of agile frameworks
- Key activities in agile operations
- Tooling – defend to respond

From incident response to agile security operations engineering

In this section, we will develop the framework for agile security operations engineering. The framework for agile security operations engineering is based on the incident loop we discussed in *Chapter 2*, *Incident Response – A Key Capability in Security Operations*, and develops the details as well as the consequences for tooling and engineering practices.

The key to going from incidents to incident response to security operations is to close the loop with a set of specific practices that ensure that organizations make the most of their incidents – when preventing, detecting, responding, and continuously managing their security posture and program.

The process starts with mapping the incident loop from the previous chapter and then defining the activities that turn the loop from an *incident* into a cybersecurity *program*.

> **It's not agile**
>
> This chapter develops an agile approach to security operations that is agile in the sense that it rapidly adapts and predicts fast-moving environments and situations. It is not agile in the sense that it strictly adheres to a specific underlying methodology that is commonly used in agile software development such as Scrum or Kanban, although it learns from and takes the best of these frameworks to target the four objectives of incident response we mentioned in the previous chapters.
>
> Therefore, some may argue that the framework in this chapter is not agile. Viewed from the perspective of strict adherence to frameworks, it isn't. But in terms of developing a tactical framework in which security teams can defend their organizations during cyber attacks while enabling the flexibility, effectiveness, and capability to respond to rapidly changing situations during attacks, it is agile.
>
> A good website to consult while reading this chapter is the Agile Alliance (`https://www.agilealliance.org/`), which contains resources and a glossary of the most important terms. Keep in mind that in this book, we'll repurpose the agile approach to suit security operations.
>
> The best security teams have already operated on agile principles for a while. The framework developed in this chapter loosely derives from a talk by Frode Hommedal at the First.org TC in Oslo, 2015 that, to my knowledge, is no longer available on the internet.

The key step in that process is closing the incident loop, which is an abbreviated way of saying that a structured set of activities must exist that enable an organization to learn from an incident and improve its detection and response capabilities.

Such an approach has significant advantages. In many cases, incidents are *Pareto optimizable*, which means that the large number of attacks that organizations experience fall into a small number of categories. Accelerating the response for the categories of the most frequent attacks and incidents will pay significant dividends in reducing the workload of the security team.

Mapping the incident loop

In *Chapter 2*, *Incident Response – A Key Capability in Security Operations*, we discussed the incident response loop and why an agile approach in incidents is needed. The incident loop consists of six phases: preparation, identification (which we broke down into detection and analysis), containment, eradication, recovery, and lessons learned.

The problem with these loop approaches is that they can become a hamster wheel of pain. *Lessons learned* as the last step does not necessarily imply that security posture, defense capability, and response agility will improve. Hence, just having a *lessons learned* step to close the incident loop is insufficient to guarantee that we will be better off.

Feedback – closing the incident loop

If just *lessons learned* is not the optimal model for how we close the incident loop, we need to specify what *is* (in other words, what needs to change because of the incident). Agile security operations are looking for the specific patterns that allow organizations to not only *learn* from but also *improve* upon how incidents are handled. In addition, organizations learn about important aspects of the *motivation* of attackers and can use this to update their threat intelligence.

Closing the incident loop in agile security operations entails three specific requirements:

- Improving the *prevention* measures against the type of attack that was just experienced, such as by improving the architecture, hardening the existing infrastructure, vulnerability management, and either disabling unused and aging infrastructure or mitigating the risk around it

- Improving *detection* of attacks like the one we just experienced, such as by using detection engineering or replacing poor detective software for better quality

- Improving *responses* to the attack that we just experienced by automating and streamlining the response and communication processes, to optimize the quality and speed of the response.

These three improvements require structured learning out of our incidents, especially around attacker **tactics, techniques, and procedures (TTPs)**.

TTPs are aligned with the *business model* of an attacker and outline how an attacker drives their actions for objectives. Improvements in prevention, detection, and response should be driven by TTPs rather than low-value indicators such as IOCs, file hashes, DNS names, or similar attributes. Attackers change these quite frequently, whereas the business model of an attacker – how they aim to achieve their objectives – is much harder to change.

Sometimes, this hierarchy of data is referred to as the **pyramid of pain**, a term introduced in a blog post by David Bianco: `http://detect-respond.blogspot.com/2013/03/the-pyramid-of-pain.html`. The idea of the pyramid of pain is that a robust understanding of the business model of an attacker and the behavior of their tools on your network leads you to more effective use of indicators.

> **Example – APTs and Incident Response**
>
> Around 2015-2018, the term **Advanced Persistent Threat (APT)** was used a lot in marketing material, where the customer was led to focus on the *advanced* aspect of the APT, whereas the component that needs to be focused on is *persistent*. Since APTs are persistent, prevention, detection, and response methods must be improved after attacks using information gleaned from past attacks.

Dealing with adversaries often benefits greatly from the ability to develop specific TTPs about an attack, and hence on the robust process of closing the incident loop, as we will advocate in this chapter.

As an example, attackers often work in the time zone of their residence, or with keyboard layouts matching their country of origin. This can be a useful TTP. Similarly, some attackers like to mostly register their DNS names with the same registrar or use specific **top-level domain (TLD)** names for their activities. Another useful TTP is tooling or details around the initial attack vector, such as the mail domains where initial emails are being sent from, if the initial intrusion vector is email..

With attacks becoming more businesslike in terms of their objectives, attackers also operate more like businesses.

The businesslike weaknesses of attackers

It is a somewhat common misconception that attackers are either loners or highly organized state-sponsored actors. The cybercrime scene has evolved into a highly specialized set of businesses, with malware developers, exploit traders, people handling customer interactions, and monetization all forming an organized cybercriminal ecosystem that operates much like a modern business. This leads to specific weaknesses of cyber-attackers, such as the need to rely on standardized business models, limited tooling providers, adhering to common working hours, having cost-optimized business models that rely on repeatability (and thus predictability) of processes and procedures, and an ongoing need for revenue.

Research done by the endpoint security firm CrowdStrike for their Global Threat Report 2021 shows an interconnected web of malware families and actors that have defined economic relationships.

CrowdStrike divides the ecosystem into services, such as malware development and packing, credit card testing, development of phish kits, loaders and packers, and infrastructure hosting; distribution, such as spamming and social media; and monetization, which focuses on ransom negotiations, muling, money laundering, and cryptocurrency services.

Understanding the business model of an attacker allows security teams to devise defenses that break that model. This dynamic will be discussed in greater depth in *Chapter 8, Red, Blue, and purple teaming.*

A brief discussion of agile frameworks

In *Chapter 2, Incident Response – A Key Capability in Security Operations*, we defined the beginnings of an agile framework for security operations. It is now time to build that framework out to a fully fledged capability framework that implements the necessary components of agile security operations.

Agile, as a method, is primarily used in software development, and it can use several different underlying frameworks to enable the agile development of software. In this section, we aim to briefly review them and develop an idea of their possible use in incident response and security operations. The frameworks we will cover have been developed with a view to software and product development, not for incident response. However, they do contain useful information for an incident response process.

In this section, we will briefly look at the main ones before developing a framework that is ideally suited to incident response and security operations.

Lean

The **Lean** method is closely related to the Kanban method, which we will discuss next. In Lean, teams focus on visualizing the workflow and minimizing waste. Waste is defined as, for example, time spent on any product for which there is no need, or time spent on rework, task switching, waiting for others, unnecessary features, and handoffs.

Lean minimizes waste by rearchitecting the development process away from large upfront designs, instead of optimizing learning through experimentation and aiming to make consequential design commitments as late as possible (also known as keeping your options open).

Another key concept from Lean is the **minimum viable product** (**MVP**), which we can define as a version of the product that gives the team the maximum amount of learning about the customer's interaction with a product with the least effort. For instance, an MVP may consist of a landing page with mockup reports or rely on a manual process behind the scenes.

The approaches stressed by Lean certainly resonate in the realm of security operations. A Lean approach to defense stresses the rapid development of many different defenses with rapid feedback loops, which is an approach that is useful during the detection, analysis, and containment phases of an incident.

Interlude – Why having many detections working together is better

Imagine having the following choice: you can implement a super-magic security tool that is 99% effective against any attack (that is, it alerts on 99 out of 100 attacks), or you can implement two tools that are both 95% effective (that is, they alert on 95 out of 100 attacks). Which is better?

If you put the two tools in *parallel*, the tools work together, but independently of each other, on a data feed. Each of them gives a verdict on whether malicious activity is occurring in this feed. If you, as the operator, give an alert each time *one* of the tools detects something as malicious, the overall effectiveness is 1 minus 0.0025, or 99.9975. This arrangement is attractive because a tool with 95% effectiveness is usually orders of magnitude cheaper than a single tool with high effectiveness, and two of these tools will still be cheaper than a single highly effective tool.

This is a crude calculation that relies on several assumptions, but it gives you the general picture.

Kanban

The **Kanban** philosophy is all about managing the flow, limiting the **work in progress** (**WIP**), and visualizing the progress of the work. The philosophy of Kanban is to minimize work in progress and multitasking, which slows down the flow and leads to waste, both in terms of time and resources. All the work is mapped on a Kanban board under specific columns.

Kanban also introduces the concept of pull, meaning that teams pull in work according to their capacity, rather than it being pushed to them via a ticketing system, production belt, or supervisor. This notion is important, as we will see later, and radically new for most security teams, who get their incidents via an ever-increasing alert stream that threatens to overwhelm the team.

One of the elements of Kanban is that teams can develop a **definition of done**, which is a *shared understanding of expectations that must be met by software or a product when the team finishes further work on that feature*. A definition of done does not always have to mean that a feature is complete.

Scrum

Scrum is a structured method for operating software and product development teams that optimizes for speed of development and feedback on earlier releases. The rapid feedback that is emphasized by the Scrum process is vital for good incident response.

Scrum is highly structured and prescriptive, and primarily a framework for managers of teams. Scrum focuses on a limited time horizon and defines its cadence in terms of predefined **sprints**, during which the team goes through **rituals** that are also extensively documented and prescribed.

Scrum also uses the notion of team *pull* rather than push and relies on teams themselves defining which requests from the *backlog* will be pulled by the team for each *sprint*.

Some of the key scrum artifacts will be useful for this chapter are as follows:

- **User story**: The user story is a description of a small piece of functionality that an end user needs in a piece of software. It is usually captured in the form of a sentence: *As a user of <application> I need to do <something> so that <result or objective of the improvement or functionality>*. After creation, the user story is put on the backlog.

- **Task**: Tasks can be related to user stories (such as *implement this functionality*) but can also be related to things the team needs, such as new development tools, environments, or security reviews. All the tasks go on the backlog.

- **Backlog**: A list of all the work that needs to be done by the team.

- **Sprint**: A defined period in which a team seeks to complete several tasks, which are pulled by the team from the backlog.

- **Sprint backlog**: The tasks pulled by the team from the backlog, to be completed in the current sprint.

- **Increment**: A potentially shippable new version of the product or software that contains the functionality related to the user stories that have been pulled in the most recent sprint.

- **Sprint review**: The sprint review reviews the output of the sprint in terms of the product and is also used to collaborate with the product owners on what to do next.

- **Sprint retrospective**: The retrospective focuses on the processes, individual interactions, communication, processes, and tools used during the sprint and focuses on improving the team's effectiveness.

Perhaps not that surprisingly, Scrum as a framework is less suitable for incident response for several reasons:

- Scrum (along with the other methodologies) focuses on product and software development, not on responding to incidents.

- Scrum is heavily structured and lacks some of the flexibility required to adapt to attacker behavior. In general, during an incident, a team does not get the opportunity to define a sprint; the cadence is set by events and is outside of the control of the responder.

- Scrum is driven by the cadence of specific sprints that are set in advance. In an incident response process, we do not usually get to choose the cadence, but it is driven by both the attacker and the cadence of detection and analysis.

> **Scrum**
>
> The www.scrum.org website contains a lot of useful information about the scrum framework and its key components.

With that, as we will see later, the Scrum framework contains a lot that can be repurposed in the context of incident response, and the artifacts that form part of the Scrum framework can be repurposed for the process of agile security operations.

In addition to these three frameworks, many other specific frameworks fit with the agile manifesto and are used in various organizations to good effect. For this book, however, there is little value in providing detailed evaluations of all that is possible.

None of the methods that are used for software and product development translate immediately into what is needed for Agile security operations.

The following table maps out some of these models and what the requirements for agile security operations are:

	Lean	Kanban	Scrum	Security Operations
Philosophy	Minimize waste	Visibility of work in progress	Speed of development	Assumed compromise
Cadence	No particular cadence	No particular cadence	Determined by the Sprint	Determined by the attacker (predictable to some degree)
Metrics	Quality Time to market	Work in progress Estimate of lead time	Velocity Burndown chart	Ability to stop an attacker before they achieve their objectives, limit lateral movement, and learn
Methodology	Optimize the flow of products throughout the entire system	Kanban board depicting the flow	Planned sprints with defined rituals and review and retrospective sessions that follow a tight structure	Develop and extend the incident response loop as the core of security operations

Table 3.1 – Evaluation of the available Agile methodologies

Agile security operations are not necessarily committed to any of the Lean, Kanban, or Scrum models. Instead, we will focus on the specific process of incident response, some of the agile practices for the methods we discussed previously, and then design an agile security operations process that is based on closing the incident loop, ensuring that an organization can improve its security posture based on a deep understanding of the incidents that have occurred, as well as an understanding of what has already occurred.

Agile security operations

The purpose of agile security operations is to provide processes and procedures that ensure that the effectiveness of the organization during the incident loop is monitored and optimized. The critical difference between *agile* and *agile security operations* is that in agile software methodologies, we are dealing with code and environments, and, most importantly, a product. *In security operations, we are dealing with attackers who have a specific set of objectives, capabilities, and tools that are being used in an adversarial context.* Despite the use of the word agile in both cases, this makes agile security operations unique and different in terms of quality regarding agile software development.

Agile security operations have *requirements* along the following dimensions:

- **Philosophy**: The key philosophy of agile security operations is one of assumed compromise. We do not only assume that adversaries exist outside our network, but we also assume they already have a foothold. All that is necessary is for us to discover them.

- **Cadence**: Attacks follow a cadence that depends on the attacker and their speed of movement. **Advanced Persistent Threat** (**APT**) attackers are *persistent*, with attacks following a businesslike production schedule for compromise. Cadence is also influenced by the lateral movement of the attackers.

- **Key metrics**: The key metrics of the agile security operations process are related to whether an organization can successfully handle a cyber attack before the attackers reach their objectives, and how efficiently they then evict those attackers, as well as become more successful at dealing with subsequent attacks from the same group.

- **Methodology**: Agile security operations rely on limiting the number of alerts that analysts are working on, the transparency of what they are doing, and rapidly responding to important intrusions. This is, of course, the primary role of a SIEM, but agile security operations take this a step further by improving the processes by means of which alerts are handled by using automation and orchestration for standard alerts, leaving time for the events and incidents that require the most attention because they pose the largest threat and hence the most risk.

The following diagram provides a high-level overview of the incident loop, optimized for agile security operations:

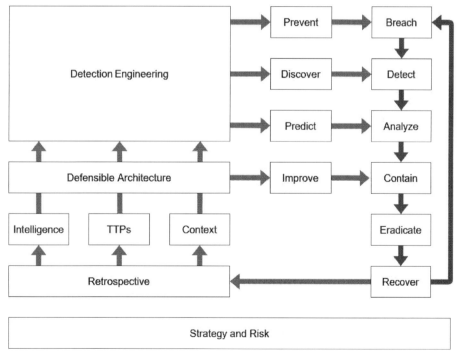

Figure 3.1 – The Agile incident loop that drives security operations .
The loop on the right is the incident response hamster wheel.

One way to think about this diagram is that it expands the *prepare* and *lessons learned* stages of the incident response loop. Specifically, agile security operations define a method for structured learning and improvement from cyber incidents that *closes the incident loop*, in ways that put an organization in a better position post-breach than it was pre-breach.

> **Principles for security operations**
>
> Agile methodologies such as Kanban and Scrum give a lot of autonomy and authority to teams to determine what problems to work on and how fast. Hence, it is key that teams work from a robust set of principles to ensure that they use the autonomy and authority with integrity and to a high standard. In these methodologies, management places a high amount of trust in individual teams.
>
> One of the best books on operative principles in business and life is Ray Dalio's book *Principles*, together with the website `https://www.principles.com`, where you can also find additional materials related to the book.
>
> I have collected some of the key principles for security operations in my book *Principles for Cybersecurity Operations*, (2020), which you may read as a companion volume to this one. It outlines the principles that I have found useful in managing security teams and resolving incidents. These principles are summarized in the *Appendix* section.

Key activities in agile security operations

In this section, we will focus on the key activities in agile security operations and the approaches and tooling they require. How we specify the activities in the agile incident loop will determine what tooling a security team requires.

This section will only contain the summaries of the relevant activities. More details will be provided in *Sections 2* and *3* of this book, especially in *Chapter 6, Active Defense*.

Breach

The philosophy of agile security operations is that a breach is eternal, and that incident response is an ongoing process. With that, it is important to realize that not all breaches are created equal. Breaches follow a cadence that is primarily determined by the attacker as they move to our environment. The cadence itself is determined by the kill chain which was discussed in the previous chapter. Our visibility of that cadence is limited by our capability to observe this movement.

Determinants of a cyber attack

In 2014, two economists from the University of Michigan, Robert Axelrod, and Rumen Iliev, studied the tactical factors that led to the timing of a cyber conflict, given that nation states have a stockpile of unused zero-day exploits. Axelrod and Iliev found that the timing of a digital attack can be determined using a model from economics that uses the following information:

- **Persistence**: How long will my target be vulnerable to the vulnerability I'm planning to use? Sooner or later, my target will patch or apply workarounds to their vulnerabilities, making my vulnerability useless.

- **Stealth**: Can my target detect this? A zero-day is not very useful if a target can detect its use.

- **Threshold**: What conditions would lead to the use of a cyber attack vector? Is it worth using on this target? Attackers hate resource waste – in this case, expensive zero-days – as much as defenders do and will generally try to use a tool that just does the job, rather than something that is overkill.

See Axelrod and Iliev: *Timing of cyber conflict* PNAS 111 (4) 1298-1303 (2014); https://doi.org/10.1073/pnas.1322638111.

Detect

The key problem for many security teams is that the number of alerts overwhelms the available resources in the team. This is the well-known phenomenon of alert fatigue.

Many teams reach for automation to lower their workload. The problem with using automation is that it can deal with standard detection and incidents but may fail to cope with tasks that require a non-standard, highly contextual, deep understanding of sophisticated (and sometimes even not so sophisticated) attacks. Automation may even lead to an ever-increasing list of alerts if it is not configured well; that is, if the automation is geared toward creating even more alerts.

Machine learning may help here but its effect is somewhat unclear. At best, it adds more high-fidelity detections. Consequently, the introduction of machine learning should replace some of the existing detections with better ones.

At worst, machine learning may add a new category of mathematically anomalous but potentially irrelevant detections and alerts to the stream. This makes the problem worse in many ways. The detection from machine learning requires more work to investigate (because it is not initially clear what triggers them) and a thorough analysis of cause and effect is more difficult with machine learning algorithms.

Pull events instead of push

Here is a radical question: why do security teams not *pull* detection events instead of having an overwhelming number of tickets opened for them? This will allow a team to focus on useful alerts that can be investigated in more depth, contextualized, and updated according to the detection engineering process.

On the face of it, that seems like a crazy idea. Alerts indicate potential security incidents; shouldn't they *all* be investigated? However, incidents often generate many alerts, all of which are related to the same incident. The size of the alert stream may be misleading. The idea of pulling detections relies on the idea that the team itself will have the best understanding of what constitutes alerts worth their time.

In many cases, alerts that do not seem all that serious lead us to more interesting intrusions, while also explaining many related aspects of the alert stream.

It is still an open question regarding how this should be done: security teams should not miss events and should be alert regarding what goes on in these alert streams. At the same time, automated alert generation may only adapt to new types of attacks with difficulty and certainly won't adapt without active intervention. From this perspective, a team of analysts can be tasked with performing *daily tasks* and responding to standard alerts, while a team of threat hunters or purple teamers may work on dedicated alert pulling and investigation of new types of attack. This will be discussed in more depth in *Chapter 8, Red, Blue, and Purple Teaming*.

A security team that has a good handle on the quality of the alerts that it receives will quickly be able to identify the most promising ones, and then spend the right amount of effort on each one.

Pulling alerts should happen with a high degree of trust and integrity in the security team. Here, a few basic rules should be followed:

- Define *criticality* based on the criticality of a process, rather than a system.
- Define *relationships* with other alerts or alert families and place an alert in a specific context.
- Define the *scope* and *priority* of the investigation, as well as how much time can be spent on it before a decision is made to either continue or abandon the investigation.

The approach to detection and response will be discussed in more detail in *Chapter 8, Red, blue, and purple teaming*.

Analyze

Analyzing a detection involves getting the additional context around an alert to decide whether an *alert is a true positive or false positive* (an alert has, of course, already happened at this point).

Analysis involves looking at the specific conditions that the alert has occurred in, as well as looking up additional information on other systems. For instance, when a malware detection event occurs, we may want to consider the DNS logs or system logs to determine whether the malware managed to run and whether it managed to establish, for instance, command and control.

For security operations, analysis must happen quickly and reliably, and to that end, organizations need to ensure that their security teams have sufficient visibility as well as searchability of logs.

Logging strategy

Specifically, organizations should consider implementing a **logging strategy**, which determines which system and application logs are collected, how they are stored, and how they will be searched. A logging strategy for security needs to be driven from an understanding of what constitutes a security event, and then you must work backward from there to determine what logs should be collected and how. In addition, compliance requirements may determine what logs are collected and how long they are kept.

Modern SIEMs allow a team to capture this information and apply it across the data being ingested by the SIEM to determine when a sequence of events becomes a security incident.

> **Windows event logging**
>
> A good example of a (generic) logging strategy for Windows systems was developed by The Australian Cybersecurity Centre, which defined specific guidance for Windows event logging and forwarding. This may serve as an initial logging strategy for Windows systems. It is available here: `https://www.cyber.gov.au/acsc/view-all-content/publications/windows-event-logging-and-forwarding`. Similarly, the benchmarks developed by the Center for Internet Security also contain logging guidelines for various environments and systems, along with various hardening guides. They are available (with free registration) from this page: `https://www.cisecurity.org/cis-benchmarks/`.

The approach and context of a logging strategy is primarily architectural, and will be discussed in more detail in *Chapter 5, Defensible Architecture*.

No single pane of glass

A common pitfall of security tooling requirements is the idea that all tooling should be accessible through a single interface. Even worse, sometimes, this is considered a critical requirement of a security tool, often in the mistaken belief that such a *single pane of glass* will assist with alert fatigue and accelerate the analysis of alerts.

It is unclear that this is money well spent. In practice, all that security teams need to perform the analysis is the ability to rapidly pivot between tools, perform ad hoc queries, and analyze the results from different tools. Therefore, the following requirements are preferable when choosing security tooling:

- Rapid pivoting gets easier if the tools have web-based interfaces with a *single authentication* system; for instance, using **OAuth** or **SAML**.

- Performing ad hoc queries implies that the tool is driven off a *data lake architecture* with loose coupling, APIs, and some analytics tooling.

- Ensure systems run from the same time source to make timelining possible.

- Ensure a *single identity* across the organization to speed up analysis and the attribution of events.

Let's proceed to the next steps.

Next steps

The outcome of the analysis step is determining whether an alert was a true positive (an alert and a security event) or a false positive (an alert but no security event). Each of these two possibilities triggers an activity:

- A *false positive* prompts us to consider whether we should update the detection and move into detection engineering.

- A *true positive* leads us to move to the next step in incident response: containment. In this case, the analysis has given us additional context and information about the event that we can use to both contain and recover from the incident.

Typically, we must determine what stage of the kill chain an attacker may have progressed to. The kill chain was outlined in *Chapter 2, Incident Response – A Key Capability in Security Operations*. The containment and eradication phases of incident response, as well as the time available to respond, rely on this information.

Contain

If the analysis reveals that an incident has occurred, the incident needs to be *contained*.

The analysis has given us additional context around the alert, as determined by the stage of the kill chain the attacker is in and has given us some further clues as to what tooling and methods are being used by an attacker.

Containment can follow a combination of the following strategies:

- **Deceive** an attacker.
- **Deny** an attacker the opportunity for further lateral movement by isolating the host or network segment that has been compromised.
- **Disrupt** the capabilities of the tooling they have already deployed.
- **Destroy** the tooling that has already been deployed, thus making it impossible for an attacker to continue.

It almost always makes sense to monitor the compromised and neighboring parts of the network with extra care after containment to make sure that an attacker is indeed contained and not running amok somewhere else.

> **Note**
>
> Research done by the firm CrowdStrike has indicated that the time from initial access to lateral movement in 2018 was about 2 hours. More detailed research even developed a league table of attackers based on their breakout time, the time it took for lateral movement to be successful: `https://www.crowdstrike.com/blog/first-ever-adversary-ranking-in-2019-global-threat-report-highlights-the-importance-of-speed/`.

To contain effectively, teams should have the authority and ability to make the necessary changes quickly. Authority is a key element of the design of security teams and should be covered before incidents in an SOC charter that defines the constituency (that is, who the security team will act for), as well as the authority of the team (that is, what they can do under what circumstances). This aspect will be discussed in more detail in *Chapter 9, Running and Operating Security Services*.

> **Authority**
>
> More information about authority in security teams may be found in
> Section 2.3.3 of Jason Zimmerman's *Ten Strategies of a World-Class SOC,*
> Mitre Corporation, 2014, available here: `https://www.mitre.org/`
> `publications/all/ten-strategies-of-a-world-class-`
> `cybersecurity-operations-center`.

Eradicate

Eradicating attackers involves removing the tooling and access that attackers have deployed on the network, as well as making sure that re-entry is not possible, at least not through the same vector.

Something to consider here, and something that good analysis should be able to give a lead on, is whether it is preferable to observe an attacker rather than eradicate them, especially in an early stage of the kill chain. Provided the attacker is contained and can be observed, this sometimes gives us a good opportunity to discover more about their intentions. However, the observation strategy needs a mature team coupled with a robust understanding of when to pull the plug on the attacker.

The requirements for eradication are as follows:

- Ensure that *all* tooling and access to an attacker is removed, not just some of it.

- Ensure that the vulnerabilities that enabled the initial attack vector (and some trivial variants of it) have been closed to prevent attackers from reentering the network.

- Write some specific alerts for attacker activity and put them into the detection system to alert on any reoccurrence of activity.

Recover

Recovery from an incident becomes easier if the attackers have not achieved their objectives because in this case, the organization has likely avoided the large data breaches, ransoms, and compromises that make recovery costly and difficult.

But also, incidents that were stopped earlier in the kill chain can be costly to recover from. For instance, an environment may need to be rebuilt in its entirety, some data may be lost, or complex changes to prevent reoccurrence may be necessary. Recovery in almost all instances is something that needs to be operationally addressed by the business. It is unlikely that it can be outsourced, and the effort involved in recovery can be significant and have significant business impact. Hence it makes sense to plan recovery activities in advance.

Develop context and TTPs

Many organizations stop the process of incident response once they have recovered from the incident, thus denying themselves the opportunity to learn from the incident and improve their defenses. Agile incident response focuses specifically on the positive feedback from learning and how this may drive improvement.

The first step in this process is to collect the work that was started in the analysis and add anything else discovered about the incident to a threat intelligence platform. This allows further events associated with the event to also be categorized under the same threat group. The threat intelligence platform in the first instance can be a simple wiki or even a document stating whether something about the incident has been kept and is searchable.

> **The naming of threat groups**
>
> Many groups are persistent, and it may help a team to develop code names for them, on the basis that these threat groups will try to compromise us many times. Having a code name assists in gathering all that activity under a single label. It is better to have such names not refer to nationalities, individuals, or national symbols, as that assumes knowledge about an attacker that is, in most cases, unsupported by the available attribution and may also prejudge future analysis. It is usually best to take something as neutral as possible but meaningful to the team, such as a reference to a memorable event during the first or second time the team responded to an incident caused by these attackers.

The incident and how it's handled may also provide useful insights into the tactics, techniques, and procedures of an attacker. This is useful to collect at the closure of an incident as well.

Updating the architecture, strategy, and risk

The incident and how it's handled can also provide useful clues for updating or improving the architecture, although generally, improvements here will take some time to work through the deployed infrastructure.

Strategy and risk calculations will also benefit from incident data as it provides an improved understanding of the adversaries that are faced by the business and the effectiveness of the current defenses.

Detection engineering

As part of our closure of an incident we can also improve detection engineering. In *Chapter 2, Incident Response – A Key Capability in Security Operations*, we discussed detection engineering as an activity that develops, tests, and applies detections based on an understanding of the business context to cyber compromises. This elicits quality control on detection code.

Detection engineering aims to reduce the number of false positives, detect as many incidents as possible promptly, and ensure that detection tools are tasked with the right information (that is, the detection is deployed to the tool that does the detection) and reviewed for fidelity. As suggested by the workflow in *Figure 2.2*, the detection engineering process consists of four specific steps:

1. **Developing the detection**: The detection is developed based on the information available from false positives, past breaches, threat intelligence, business context, or threat modeling.

2. **Storing the detection in a detection repository**: It is important to have a central repository for detection code.

3. **Tasking workflow**: This is where the detection is deployed to the tool that monitors the network, the logs, the packets on the firewall, or the files and events on endpoints.

4. Monitoring the **performance** of the deployed detection, especially the false positives and reliability of the detection.

> **Detection as code**
>
> The GitHub repository of Florian Roth, `https://github.com/ neo23x0`, contains good examples of what detection as code may look like in practice. Detection engineering is currently not something that is supported widely by most toolsets, and it will require (in the first instance) a manual rather than an automated deployment pipeline.

Improvements – prevention, discovery, and prediction

The last step of agile security operations is to improve the prevention, discovery, and prediction of future breaches. The design and implementation of improvements will be discussed in more detail in *Chapter 5, Defensible Architecture*.

Making changes to the configuration of tools that only do detection is generally low risk and should be a pre-approved change that's managed by the SOC. It is then up to the SOC to decide whether they need a **Test** and **User Acceptance Testing** (**UAT**) environment to test passive detection changes, but this should not be necessary. It will be hard to robustly test changes to detections in a test environment because this would involve having to simulate actual attacks in this environment. Such simulations are possible, but mostly for larger and well-resourced teams.

For many small teams, the deployment pipeline of detections and predictions will be a manual affair, deployed with little to no risk on the actual environment, and monitored intensively after deployment.

In the remainder of this chapter, we'll focus on some tactical comments on tooling and tool deployment by looking at automation and coverage using the MITRE Shield framework.

Tooling – defend to respond

The agile security operations process strongly influences the tools that are deployed and how they are deployed. In this section, I will briefly discuss some of the tooling for passive and active defense.

Passive defense

Passive defense tooling focuses on either blocking attackers through defenses such as access control, firewalls, and system hardening, as well as the tooling that organizations can deploy to detect an attack has occurred and analyze it. Similarly, if you wish to contain incidents, you will need passive defense tools.

The SOC nuclear triad

The security researcher Anton Chuvakin maintains that a nuclear triad of SOC tooling exists, consisting of Security Incident Event Monitoring (which, in this model, would include logging), Enterprise Detection and Response, and a capability for network detection and forensics. This is still a good model to go on: `https://blogs.gartner.com/anton-chuvakin/2015/08/04/your-soc-nuclear-triad/`. The **SOC nuclear triad** focuses on passive defense, not on how defense teams may actively engage with an attacker. More recently, he also suggested that Application Security Visibility may become the fourth pillar of the quad: `https://medium.com/anton-on-security/back-in-2015-while-working-on-a-gartner-soc-paper-i-coined-the-concept-of-soc-nuclear-triad-8961004c734`.

Passive defense tooling also needs to be managed across multiple environments, such as on-premises infrastructure, cloud, and increasingly intelligent devices. Hence, passive defense engineering is a large, growing, and complex problem that needs to be carefully considered.

To deploy and maintain all that tooling, security teams need a specific engineering function that focuses on the tools themselves. Developing and maintaining security tools is an ongoing concern, where a few guidelines apply:

- To cut down on alert fatigue and the volume of alerts, SIEM tools should seek to automate frequent high-fidelity alerts and route them immediately into the help desk system for resolution. The security team itself only maintains the oversight of these automated alerts; it does not handle them.

- Enterprise detection and response tools should implement functionality beyond antivirus and anti-malware but should have the capability to detect and record system events (such as processes that have been stopped and started). It should also include tools to rapidly isolate endpoints remotely and perform searches on an environment in the form of OSQuery or Velociraptor queries. This can help determine whether malicious artifacts are present on an endpoint. Such tools may be available open source or be part of a commercial detection and response solution. These are often referred to by the acronym XDR.

The growth in cloud environments and the growing use of encryption will potentially make network intrusion detection less useful over time, although it is still a useful tool. The placement of network sensors at strategic points in the network needs careful consideration and needs to be used when terminating network encryption.

Active defense – Mitre ATT&CK and Shield

The Mitre ATT&CK framework is a well-known framework that models attackers and attack groups based on their tooling and techniques, tactics, and procedures. The ATT&CK framework can be found here: `https://attack.mitre.org`. The tactics of the ATT&CK framework map roughly to the kill chain and are used widely in active defense and threat intelligence.

> **Note**
>
> ATT&CK is quite well documented on the `attack.mitre.org` website. An extensive chapter on ATT&CK can be found in *Practical Threat Intelligence and Data-Driven Threat Hunting*, by *Valentina Palacín, Packt*. A further discussion of ATT&CK can also be found in *Chapter 6, Active Defense*, of this book.

The tactics that make up the ATT&CK framework are as follows:

- **Reconnaissance**: The external investigation of the victim's environment to determine avenues of access and weapons that could be used to attack the victim.

- **Resource Development**: Development of the resources needed by the attacker to execute the attack.

- **Initial Access**: The initial access to the environment.

- **Execution**: Executing the payload of the cyber weapon in the victim's environment.

- **Persistence**: Ensuring that the attackers have a configured way back into the system, such as a backdoor, or an account that may be used to log back in later.

- **Privilege Escalation**: Activities to gain more access from the initial access point and elevate the authorization of the attacker or gain access to more systems.

- **Defense Evasion**: The activities to hide the attacker from defensive tooling and teams.

- **Credential Access**: Techniques to steal credentials or passwords.

- **Discovery**: Activities on the victim network that assist an attacker in discovering additional systems, or any living off-the-land tools that may be used.

- **Lateral Movement**: Activities that the attacker performs to move from the initial points of compromise to other systems in the network.

- **Collection**: Gathering information or information sources that are relevant to the attacker's objectives.

- **Command and Control**: Establishing communications between the attacker's infrastructure and the victim's infrastructure to control the victim's infrastructure.

- **Exfiltration**: Exfiltrating the data that forms part of achieving the attacker's objective. This can also involve staging, packaging, and encrypting the data to avoid detection.

- **Impact**: This category describes a list of possible impacts of a cyber attack that result from the previous tactics being successfully applied to the victim's environment.

The tactics in the ATT&CK framework can be used as guides to design and implement specific defenses that aim to thwart successful completion of this tactic. The ATT&CK framework can be combined with the Shield framework, which focuses on a range of defense tooling that is available to security teams, as well as its effectiveness against specific tactics in the ATT&CK framework. Whereas defenders can use the ATT&CK framework to analyze attacks and perform intelligence-driven incident responses, Shield is an extensive guide to tooling.

Like ATT&CK, Shield also consists of several *defensive* tactics. The focus of the Shield framework is specifically on active defense and is defined as *the employment of limited offensive action and counterattacks to deny a contested area or position* to the attacker. Various definitions can be found here: `https://shield.mitre.org/resources/getting-started`. Shield, like ATT&CK, uses the usual terminology of tactics, techniques, and procedures, but focuses them on *defensive* actions. This is, of course, entirely possible: defenders, like attackers, also have a specific arsenal of TTPs.

The focus of Shield is deception: how to divert an attacker from their real objective and drive them to an environment of the defender's choosing so that their behavior can be studied further. Such environments could be **honeypots** or **honeynets**.

The tactics that make up the Shield framework are as follows:

- **Channel**: Channel is the capability a security team may have to deceive attackers and channel them into an area of the defender's choosing, such as a decoy network or a hardened network.

- **Collect**: This term refers to the capability of a team to gather an adversary's toolset and collect other data about their activity on the network. This information may then be used to strengthen defenses or contain an attacker.

- **Contain**: This is the capability to restrict an attacker to a specific and constrained area that they cannot escape from.

- **Detect**: Detection is the capability to develop and maintain awareness of an attacker's behavior.

- **Disrupt**: Disruption prevents an attacker from completing their mission by either slowing the attacker down (increasing the time required to complete the mission) or making it harder, through system hardening or otherwise, to complete the mission.

- **Facilitate**: The facilitate step is the opposite of the disrupt step and allows an attacker to complete part of their mission. The purpose of this could be to present an attacker with a false or watermarked set of data of relatively little value.

- **Legitimize**: This activity adds authenticity to deceptive components to convince an attacker that a decoy system is real.

- **Test**: This capability studies an attacker in the wild to determine their capability, motivation, or behavior.

The Shield terminology also adds two new terms to the defense lexicon:

- **Opportunity spaces**, which are the high-level opportunities for active defense that arise when the attacker employs a specific technique.

- **Use cases**, which describe what a defender could do to take advantage of an opportunity presented by an attacker's action.

In the latter aspect, the Shield framework can be mapped to ATT&CK techniques, where the use of a particular ATT&CK technique generates an opportunity space for the defender, with specific use cases that outline what a defender might do to thwart that specific technique.

In that sense, specific Shield techniques fit with several opportunity spaces, use cases, and procedures intended to limit the effectiveness of several ATT&CK techniques.

There are two ways in which defenders can use Shield to their advantage:

- Shield provides a catalog of defensive techniques that enable active defense, and defenders can rate their current toolset and capabilities against what is required.

- During the analysis and containment phase of an incident, defenders can consult the Shield matrix to determine what their active defense options are.

Summary

In this chapter, we defined an agile framework for security operations that is centered in the incident response loop, with a specific methodology for agile security operations. This chapter has stressed that learning from incidents must lead to improvements in prevention, detection, and response practices.

An important consequence of this development is that the key tooling of security operations changes. We focused on developing a *framework* for agile security operations that specifies specific *activities* that form part of the core of agile security operations. This realignment has consequences for *engineering* and *tooling requirements* as it introduces a new set of activities and associated tools to the security team.

To free up the time to work with high profile incidents in more detail, I have proposed that, under certain conditions and in addition to the performance of daily checks, security teams should be allowed to *pull* their alerts from the queue, rather than be expected to deal with all alerts in a priority-based, first-in-first-out model. In other words, security is not a help desk.

We also discussed the importance of passive defense tooling and the *Mitre Shield* framework, which classifies and categorizes active defense tooling.

This chapter concludes *Section 1* of the book. In *Section 2*, we will focus on some of the underlying ideas of agile security operations, especially the principles and key concepts of defensible architecture and active defense. *Section 3* will then fill in some of the remaining gaps. In the next chapter, we will discuss some of the key concepts of resilience and dive deeper into concepts that shape incidence response.

Section 2: Defensible Organizations

Part 2 discusses the nebulous topic of "security culture" and "defensible organizations." I approach security culture from the viewpoint of a number of key security concepts: chaos, constraints, defensibility, exaptation, strategy, and tactics, and illustrate how these play a role in security culture. I then move on to lay out the basic concepts of defensible architecture and defensible operations. By "defensible" in this context, I mean that these are capable of surviving a modern cyber attack. I then move on to discuss how we can test these notions through gamification and wargaming.

This part of the book comprises the following chapters:

- *Chapter 4, Key Concepts in Cyber Defense*
- *Chapter 5, Defensible Architecture*
- *Chapter 6, Active Defense*
- *Chapter 7, How Secure Are You? – Measuring Security Posture*

4
Key Concepts in Cyber Defense

In *Chapter 1, How Security Operations Are Changing*, and *Chapter 2, Incident Response – A Key Capability in Security Operations*, we argued that security operations are at the core of a security program, and that incident response is at the core of security operations. Moreover, we argued that an **agile** framework is preferred for both security operations and incident response, and we made a proposal for such a framework.

However, incidents are often confusing for the handler, with competing data, interpretations of data, and a multitude of events to analyze. The relatively static models of the life cycle are sometimes difficult to apply in these circumstances. Hence, in this chapter, we will widen the scope of our skillset to include tools that offer a broader perspective.

Cybersecurity is rife with military acronyms, unhelpful analogies, and failed models for defense. The problem is that most of the time, the key concepts of cyber defense are not considered or well considered by defenders, and the gap created is filled with language and models borrowed from the defense industry and the intelligence world. This makes for interesting mystifications about cybersecurity.

The purpose of this chapter will be to replace unhelpful analogies and models with ones that are informative and functional. Hence, this chapter is unlike most of what you will ever read in a book about cybersecurity.

This chapter will introduce the key concepts that make up the culture and ethos of agile security: **chaos**, **constraints**, **defensibility**, **strategy**, and **tactics**. We will focus on how to apply these terms correctly.

This chapter will use the concept of the **Cynefin** framework to delve deeper into these concepts and how they shape thinking during incident response. The Cynefin framework has been developed to deal with situations such as security incidents, where the available data may be confusing, certainty is lacking, a direction needs to be set with insufficient information, and someone needs to make sense of it all in a hurry. From that perspective, it is a sensemaking framework.

Specifically, this chapter will cover the following topics:

- What is cyber defense?
- How our love for failed models sets cybersecurity up for failure.
- How and why we are playing a discoordination game in cyber defense.
- Coordination and discoordination.
- A framework for dealing with uncertainty – the Cynefin framework and how it applies to cyber operations.
- Structured analytic techniques.
- Security skillset.

What is cyber defense?

The view we have developed up until now is that effective cyber defense is a credible and consistent capability in an organization to perform incident response when under cyberattack. The key point is what we understand by *credible* in this context.

The four aims of incident response were stated in *Chapter 1, How Security Operations Are Changing*. The most important one is that incident response is effective enough that attackers cannot achieve their objectives and eventually are forced to leave empty-handed. On that criterion, the current state of cyber-operations in many organizations leaves things to be desired.

Enduring failure

If the world's collective cybersecurity operations had a military code name, it would be *Enduring failure*. Unfortunately, in cybersecurity, we are fond of military code names and jargon. In this section, I will argue against several deep-seated but ultimately unhelpful analogies and failed models.

One of the unhelpful analogies is to think of cybersecurity incidents as analogous to acts of war, leading us to believe that response and defense are also military-oriented. That overlooks the fact that, in cybersecurity, we are more interested in defense than offense.

A similarly unhelpful and closely related analogy is that our security designs should resemble those of a fortress, with **defense in depth**, gatehouses, and guards.

The reason these unhelpful analogies matter is because they enable strategic miscalculation. If we think cybersecurity is like some sort of warfare, then an attractive strategy is to militarize the internet and look upon it as a *theater of war* rather than as a public sphere. This is a costly mistake, not only financially, but primarily in terms of opportunity.

Offense and Defense

In a 2015 report for the Atlantic Council, Jason Healey argues that the internet security community is *offense*-focused to the detriment of *defense*. According to Healey, the origin of this trend is a situation where "*The military and intelligence agencies of the US government can classify their work away from public scrutiny and (compared to agencies working on digital innovation or cybersecurity) have significantly larger budgets, fewer interagency hurdles, friendlier oversight committees in Congress, more and better trained personnel, relatively mature bureaucratic processes, long-term planners, and risk-seeking leadership supported by lawyers who want to get to "yes." This focus on offense leads to a situation where the Department of Homeland Security, the overall cyber defense lead in the US, employs around 1500 people versus estimates of 66000 to 88000 people working in cyber offense*" (*p 20*). This situation has not materially changed since the report was written, which can be accessed in full at the following link:

```
https://www.atlanticcouncil.org/wp-content/
uploads/2015/08/AC_StrategyPapers_No8_Saving_
Cyberspace_WEB.pdf
```

Most commercial organizations are not prepared for a future in which the security of their networks becomes a primarily military affair. But, considering the five types of cyber defense we discussed in *Chapter 1*, *How Security Operations Are Changing*, there may be a state role to play for the *offense* type of defense, in which a state employs legal methods such as international law and policing treaties to address cybersecurity risks at a national level.

A final unhelpful analogy, again closely related to the miscalculation that cybersecurity is analogous to warfare, is that offense is the best defense. This is sometimes also called a *defend forward* strategy.

The purpose of an offense-focused defense is to go after your adversaries and *defend forward*. This strategy places a lot of value in complex and large-scale take-down operations for botnets and adversaries. However helpful these activities are in the battle against cybercriminals, they are limited in value when it comes to deciding what organizations can and should do to further their cyber defense.

Cyber War Will Not Take Place

In a 2013 book, Thomas Rid argues that cyber war will not take place. His idea is that the conditions of Clausewitz's definition of war are difficult to meet with cyber aims. As Rid argues, cyber will support espionage and sabotage, but it is hard to go beyond that. All these aspects of cyberwar point to a de-escalation of tension, not an increase. For his full discussion of these ideas, see *Cyber War Will Not Take Place*, Thomas Rid, Oxford University Press.

Cyber vendors are often fond of the famous Sun Tzu quote, "*If you know the enemy and know yourself, you need not fear the result of a hundred battles. If you know yourself but not the enemy, for every victory gained you will also suffer a defeat. If you know neither the enemy nor yourself, you will succumb in every battle,*" from *The Art of War*.

Superior knowledge of our own environments is indeed a key element in effective cyber defense, but it is an open question as to how this is best done.

Asset Management

From the viewpoint that superior knowledge of your own environment is a key element of effective defense, many cyber frameworks call for asset management as a first activity in setting up a cyber program. This is somewhat problematic. While asset management is important in the general sense that *you cannot defend what you don't know you have*, the problem with asset management as a *first* step in cyber defense is that it prompts organizations to believe that they must have a large **Configuration Management Database** (**CMDB**) or similar installation to effectively defend their assets. Implementation and ongoing maintenance of these CMDBs often fails in practice.

The asset management bar for successful defense is much lower. What matters most is not the full *management* of all assets, but rather the timely *visibility* or even *discoverability* of assets. A good rule to have is that *assets are discoverable in a time frame that matters for the resolution of an incident*. Typically, the time frame is somewhat dependent on the incident, and this means a duration of about 10 minutes.

Rather than focusing on a large technology implementation, most organizations would be better off investing in *visibility* and *discoverability*.

Perhaps even more important than knowledge of our own environment is the way we choose to conduct cyber defense.

The key focus of our concept of cyber defense is to limit the offensive *options* and *survival time* of attackers on our network. To do that, we do not need fortresses, offensive actions, or large-scale, Hollywood-style operations against cyber gangs.

We need a *defense first*-oriented approach that has the following characteristics:

- The ability to quickly make sense of a situation that is confusing and bewildering. In this chapter, we will discuss the Cynefin framework as a sense-making framework

- The ability to move quickly through confusion and chaos. In this chapter, we discuss some of the techniques discussed in Dave Snowden and Allessandro Rancati's small book, *Managing complexity (and chaos) in times of crisis* (`https://publications.jrc.ec.europa.eu/repository/handle/JRC123629`).

- The ability to process large volumes of data quickly and reliably. In this chapter, we discuss how structured analytic techniques may be used to that effect.

In this defense-first approach, it is important that we are clear about how our security operations fit our needs, as well as the differences between strategy, tactics, operations, and technical matters.

The fit of security operations

Despite the importance of cybersecurity, there is still not a lot of consideration given to the conceptual background that drives its strategy, tactics, and operations.

Many organizations mistakenly believe that having a strategy means having a compliance-driven program and that little else matters. On the other hand, equally many security professionals object to being called tactical.

Broadly speaking, the difference between strategy, tactics, and operations is widely misunderstood among cybersecurity practitioners.

This lack of understanding is generally compounded by a serious confusion in what constitutes good **security leadership**.

> **What Is Strategy?**
>
> In *Chapter 6* of *Strategy: A History*, Lawrence Freedman illustrates that the focus on strategy versus tactics only came into focus in the early nineteenth century, against a backdrop where the thinking about battles changed from a *chance of arms* (which was the conduct of battle up to 1820) to a battle of *annihilation* that would be capable of determining the future political alignment between great powers. Strategy thus became the means by which a decisive battle could be used to shape the future of international statecraft.
>
> *Strategy: A History, Lawrence Freedman, Oxford University Press.*

In cybersecurity, it is somewhat common for the focus between strategic, tactical, and operational factors to become muddled. The difficulties the cybersecurity profession has with the difference between strategy and tactics is reflected in the debate between tactical versus strategic **Chief Information Security Officers** (**CISOs**) and the wrongheaded notion, popular at times, that being strategic is often preferable in some way to being tactical. Especially damaging is the notion that being tactical is being reactive.

> **Types of CISO**
>
> An interesting observation by the executive search firm **Heidrick and Struggles** is that security leadership comes in many forms and varieties, and an organization needs an understanding of their own security needs and the shape of the threat landscape to structure their security function:
>
> ```
> https://www.heidrick.com/en/insights/
> cybersecurity/upending_tradition_modeling_
> tomorrows_cybersecurity_organization
> ```
>
> CISOs can come in different varieties, from having a technology or product focus to having a risk and compliance focus.

Robust security operations need to play solidly across the four layers of strategic, tactical, operational, and technical considerations, and an organization's cybersecurity professionals should have a sound understanding of the following:

- **Strategic**: The strategic layer focuses proactively on the integration of security into the business strategy and business processes. The focus is on the future program as it needs to take shape in the future of the business, as well as the roadmap to that future state. This is captured in the security strategy.

- **Tactical**: The tactical layer focuses reactively on optimizing the outcomes for the business with the opportunities already available to the defender, as well as on the core reactive skill of incident response. Tactics also play a key role in informing strategy about gaps and misalignment in the current defensive measures.

- **Operational**: The operational layer is proactively focused on the identification of threats and the opportunities that an organization may present to an adversary, as well as on tool selection, team structure, strengths, and weaknesses.

- **Technical**: The technical layer focuses on the technical tools, their architecture, implementation, and operation, both proactively and reactively.

It should be clear that a comprehensive security program needs to be credible in all these layers, as well as in the interplay between them. In a good security program, there is no need for debates about whether a tactical or strategic security leader is preferable; the program needs to cover four areas exceedingly well.

Structuring security leadership

When structuring teams, most organizations focus on the organizational chart as an organizational model, and the four areas above do not immediately map to an organizational chart. Unfortunately, organizational charts are what most people working in organizational leadership and resourcing understand best.

An example organizational chart was developed in a study conducted by **Carnegie Mellon University (CMU)** in 2016. This study recommends that the CISO **reporting structure** consists of the following four organizational units:

- **Program management**: Program management looks at governance, risk and compliance, assurance, and the management of security implementation such as tooling, user training, and third-party suppliers.

- **Security operations**: The security operations unit focuses on threat monitoring, log and alert analysis, and situational awareness and handles the technical aspects of incident response such as detection, analysis, forensics, containment, and recovery.

- **Incident planning**: Incident planning focuses on how to manage high-impact incidents, and develops plans for incident response, exercises, incident retrospectives, and investigations, especially on the operational and tactical level.

- **Security engineering**: Security engineering focuses on the technical implementation of security tools and identity tools.

The full document is available here:

```
https://insights.sei.cmu.edu/blog/structuring-chief-
information-security-officer-ciso-organization/
```

In the CMU model, all four functions report to the CISO, who provides the strategic layer of the model. While the details of the remainder may vary somewhat, the tactical layer is provided primarily by both program management and incident planning, the operational layer by the leadership of security operations, and the technical layer primarily by security engineering.

Organizational charts are one example of how an organization may be structured, and since they align with how most organizations organize their human resources, they are widely used when discussing organizational structure.

However, organizational charts are not the single factor in organizational architecture. At least as important is a robust understanding of who security operations *interact* with and how. Hence, it is possible to redraw the model for security leadership based on the mapping of interactions.

An example of an alternative model for structuring security leadership is depicted in the following figure, which is based on organizational interactions, rather than reporting lines:

Figure 4.1 – A field of influence model for security leadership

In this model, the various forces shaping security are mapped with their main interfaces and along three axes. Along the bottom is the defense axis, with three of the five types of cyber defense, which were discussed in *Chapter 1, How Security Operations Are Changing*, along the bottom. The left side illustrates the roles active in security strategy and architecture, and the right side illustrates those in security operations.

Ethical principles

A question that is worth considering is what ethical principles might apply to how we conduct defensive operations, especially defensive operations that lead to effective disruptive or destructive activities that affect adversary infrastructure. The description of *ethical* as in an *ethical hacker* doesn't quite cover what is required, although it is a good start. The EC-Council provides an *Certified Ethical Hacker* program, which has an ethical statement that is based on the principle of *do no harm*, along with *legal authorization* (`https://blog.eccouncil.org/types-of-hackers-and-what-they-do-white-black-and-grey/`).

Incident responders, however, need a richer framework. A good example is provided in the academic paper *Your Botnet is My Botnet: Analysis of a Botnet Takeover*, which describes a temporary command-and-control takeover of the **Torpig botnet** by an academic research group. The botnet in question had a domain name generation algorithm for its command-and-control infrastructure, which was reverse-engineered by the researchers. Subsequently, the researchers discovered that the botnet creator had forgotten to register one of the future DNS names. The researchers registered this domain name, leading to them being able to sinkhole the botnet for about a week and monitor its operations.

> **Note**
>
> *Your Botnet is My Botnet: Analysis of a Botnet Takeover, Brett Stone-Gross, Marco Cova, Lorenzo Cavallaro, Bob Gilbert, Martin Szydlowski, Richard Kemmerer, Christopher Kruegel,* and *Giovanni Vigna,* Department of Computer Science, *University of California,* Santa Barbara, CCS'09, November 9–13, 2009, Chicago, Illinois, USA (`https://sites.cs.ucsb.edu/~chris/research/doc/ccs09_botnet.pdf`).

This botnet takeover posed an ethical dilemma. The researchers were able to tell the bots to uninstall themselves, shut the botnet down, or reconfigure the botnet during the time they operated it. In addition to making an explicit commitment to follow established legal and ethical principles, the researchers opted for the following two specific data collection principles to protect the victims:

- The sinkholed botnet should be operated so that any harm and/or damage to victims and targets of attacks would be minimized.

- The sinkholed botnet should collect enough information to enable the notification and remediation of any affected parties.

A framework for ethical principles in incident response has been compiled by the **Forum of Incidence Response and Security Teams (FIRST) Ethics Special Interest Group (SIG)** and is available at the following link:

```
https://www.first.org/global/sigs/ethics/ethics-first
```

The FIRST principles are based on the various duties that incident responders have to the victims, the wider society, and their colleagues when dealing with security incidents. The duties considered in the framework are summarized (and paraphrased) in the following section, but it is worthwhile to adopt this framework as a set of guiding principles in incident response:

- **Duty of trustworthiness**: This means that teams and team members should always behave in such a manner that it enhances trust in the team and trust between teams.

- **Duty of coordinated vulnerability disclosure**: Any vulnerabilities that are discovered should be disclosed following the coordinated disclosure process to minimize the harm associated with the disclosure. A coordinated vulnerability disclosure process is also maintained by FIRST here:

```
https://www.first.org/global/sigs/vulnerability-
coordination/multiparty/
```

- **Duty of confidentiality**: Incident information is often highly sensitive and should be kept confidential where appropriate.

- **Duty to acknowledge**: Teams should respond to any security notifications and vulnerability reports they receive from researchers and set expectations and time frames for what happens next.

- **Duty of authorization**: Teams should only perform activities on systems they are authorized to access. This also highlights the need for a **charter** for security teams that outlines this in advance of an incident.

- **Duty to inform**: Teams should keep their constituents informed about current security threats and risks.

- **Duty to respect human rights**: Teams should respect human rights in their activities.

- **Duty to team health**: Since teams have a duty to be able to continue to perform their services, they must strive to create a healthy, positive, and safe work environment that supports the physical and emotional health of all its members.

- **Duty to team ability**: The team's ability is enhanced by an environment in which learning, and experimentation are fostered.

- **Duty for responsible collection**: The collection of electronic evidence should strike a balance between the needs of incident responders and data stakeholders. Especially, data not needed for the incident analysis should be excluded from reporting. Data collected for the purposes of incident response should only be used for the purposes of incident response, and not support other purposes.

- **Duty to recognize jurisdictional boundaries**: Laws and regulations will differ in different regions, and teams should be aware of how different laws may shape their activities.

- **Duty of evidence-based reasoning**: Reporting and actions should be based on verifiable facts.

While it is good to have some examples of frameworks, teams really need to decide the relevant principles for themselves and have these documented and communicated prior to an incident.

Principles are important guidance points when teams deal with a significant amount of uncertainty. We'll deal with that in the next section.

Coordination and discoordination

Without going into the details of **game theory**, it helps to understand the situation of cyber defense teams in terms of two specific games. Cyber defense teams play a coordination game with their home constituency and a discoordination game with an attacker.

Coordination games

A **coordination game** is an engagement in which both parties (the attacker as well as the defender) have strategic options and uncertainty about the other party's behavior, but it pays to choose the same strategy.

Coordination games are the reason, for instance, why some countries drive on the left side of the road and on the right side of the road in others. Both are valid options as long as everyone follows the rules (that is, has the same strategy). Participants (players) in the traffic system (the game) coordinate (in a Road Code) which side of the road will be used, and disaster is avoided if everyone plays by the same rules.

A slightly more imaginative version of a coordination game is the following. Imagine you are parachuted into an unknown territory, but you do have a map (as shown in the following figure). You must meet someone in this territory but know neither the place nor the time. Where and when do you turn up for the meeting? Please refer to the following diagram to understand the scenario:

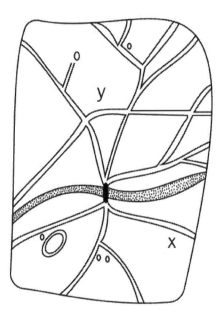

Figure 4.2 – Coordination games, where on the map would you meet? *The Strategy of Conflict*, *Thomas Schellings, Harvard University Press*

Looking at the map, it pays to turn up on the bridge at, say, noon of the day you dropped.

> **Coordination Games**
>
> This version of the coordination game is discussed in *The Strategy of Conflict*, *Thomas Schelling, Harvard University Press.*

In this classic example of a coordination game, the decision is made based on convention, expectation, and with a good degree of uncertainty.

Cyber defense teams similarly operate in such an environment when they deal with system administrators, product managers, developers, and the wider business. They have to make decisions based on convention, expectation, and sometimes allowing for significant uncertainty.

Typically, adherence to **standards** is an example of a coordination game in action. In language that we will develop more fully in the next section, standards provide a *constraint* that focuses on enabling the cooperation between security and the wider IT environment.

> **Note**
>
> The blog post by Kelly Shortridge, *Shall we play a coordination game* (2020), goes more in-depth on the notion that security can be seen to play a coordination game with the business and what this means in practice. It also illustrates that thinking in terms of games provides a rich conceptual ground for thinking about security:
>
> ```
> https://swagitda.com/blog/posts/shall-we-play-a-
> coordination-game/
> ```

While we play coordination games with our own organizations, with adversaries it is a different matter. These interactions can also be structured as a game, but instead of *coordination*, we are aiming for *discoordination*.

Discoordination games

Incident response is, in essence, a variety of **discoordination game**. In a discoordination game, one of the players tries to match the strategy of their opponent, while the other player tries to avoid matching strategies. Similarly, cyber defenders aim to *match* their strategy to that of the attacker, while the attacker tries to *avoid* the defender. It only pays for one party to play by the rules.

It is possible to subject cyber defense to economic modeling based on the notion that it is a coordination or discoordination game.

An example of what that economic modeling might look like was already outlined in *Chapter 3, Engineering for Incident Response*, where we discussed the work by Axelrod and Iliev. With the benefit of hindsight, the three factors identified by Axelrod and Iliev, **Persistence**, **Stealth**, and **Threshold**, are the ones that an elusive attacker interested in playing a discoordination game might employ.

A framework for uncertainty

Cyberattacks are characterized by uncertainty. The irony of most of the best practices in cyber defense is that we try to tackle uncertainty with known best practices. When we're up against smart and determined attackers, best practices may not be what we need. For many cyberattacks, strategy and tactics need to evolve alongside the response for defenders to match the strategy of the attacker.

We can characterize this situation as one where there is not only uncertainty but also **adversity**. That is, since the attacker and defender play a discoordination game, the attacker is intentional in their avoidance of detection, and intentionally tries to *not* play the game of the defender. In this section, I will focus on the most recent version of the Cynefin framework, developed by David Snowden as a generic management framework for handling uncertainty, and discuss specifically the role of constraints within it and use the recipes in the recent field guide as an example for managing complexity and chaos in times of crisis.

A brief overview of the Cynefin framework

A cyber-incident creates confusion and uncertainty. The focus of the Cynefin framework is to deal with *uncertainty*. The Cynefin framework was developed in 1999 by David Snowden and is used in many areas of business. Cynefin is best described as a framework that helps organizations to *make sense* of events while they are still in progress.

Sense-making is a process in which we process data and turn it into information to make it mean something. The strength of the Cynefin framework is that it distinguishes between the optimal approach for sense-making and action in several different areas: the **clear**, the **complicated**, the **complex**, and the **chaotic**. For each of these areas, there is a recommended approach to sense-making.

In this book, we will approach Cynefin as a tool that can be used during incident response.

Cynefin Background

The background of the Cynefin framework is outlined in a collection of interesting essays and in *Cynefin – Weaving Sense-Making into the Fabric of Our World, Dave Snowden, Riva Greenberg, Boudewijn Bertsch, Sue Borchardt, Sonja Blignaut,* and *Zhen Goh, Cognitive Edge* (`https://www.cognitive-edge.com/cynefinbook/`).

The following diagram represents the Cynefin framework:

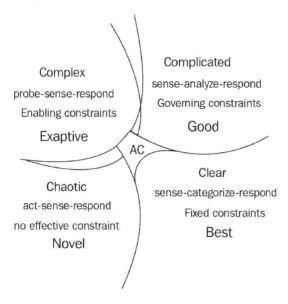

Figure 4.3 – The Cynefin framework

What makes the Cynefin framework a useful tool during incident response and also active defense, as we'll see later, is that each of these quadrants has a recommended course of action – provided we have a sense of where we are, we also have a recipe for what to do next.

The Cynefin framework has developed over time. In what follows, I will adhere to the latest version, updated in 2020 in a series of blog posts by Dave Snowden. The 2020 version revises some of the language and is also drawn somewhat differently to previous versions.

> **Note**
>
> An extensive amount of information and links can be found on the Cynefin wiki at https://www.cynefin.io and on the **Cognitive Edge** website, where I recommend you follow the blog of Dave Snowden (https://www.cognitive-edge.com/).

At a high level, the Cynefin framework consists of a separation between *ordered*, *disordered*, and *chaotic* domains. The two ordered domains are on the right-hand side (between the *clear* and *complicated* domains in the picture). The essence of an ordered domain is that we can make sense of it through observation, and then either use categorization (for example, *this is just another spam email*) or analysis (for example, *this is a highly sophisticated spear-phishing email*) to respond to the event. The *clear* domain is the domain of best practice, and, broadly speaking, the *complicated* domain is the domain of the *OODA loop*.

> **The OODA Loop**
>
> The **OODA loop** represents a cycle of **observe, orient, decide,** and **act**. It was developed by the US Air Force and is sometimes used as a tool in incident response. The OODA loop is a structured approach to the sense-categorize-respond and sense-analyze-respond categories of the Cynefin framework and is suited to known problems and small variations thereof. In the *complex* and *chaotic* domains, the OODA loop prescribes the wrong recipe.

The *complex* domain is characterized by the need to experiment, observe, fail safely, and eventually respond. At some point, activities in the complex domain may lead us to good practice and eventually best practice, in which case we gradually move from the complex (unordered) domain into one of the ordered domains. In cybersecurity operations, the complex domain is ideally suited to **threat hunting** and **detection engineering**.

In the *chaotic* domain, there is too much going on at once, and stabilizing action is immediately needed. There is a steep drop (represented by the hook-like line at the bottom of *Figure 4.3*) that represents the situation where best practice can collapse into a chaotic situation in which nothing works.

The Cynefin framework prioritizes action for each of the four quadrants:

- **Clear**: In the clear quadrant, the recommended course of action is known as *sense, categorize, respond*. Sensing is to observe what is going on, that is, to get a sense of our bearings and orient ourselves to our surroundings. Categorization places the situation in a box we already know, and we can then proceed to a scripted response. A good example of this in the cybersecurity realm is the receipt of a spam email or standardized SIEM alert. We do know how to recognize one, and we also know what to do once we have recognized one.

- **Complicated**: In the complicated quadrant, the recommended approach is known as *sense, analyze, respond*. In the complicated domain, we are dealing with situations that have not been encountered before, but where a recipe to resolve the situation may be developed with tools that already exist. An example of this in the cyber realm is when we move from receiving a standard spam message to a spear-phishing message. The latter is more complicated, and it may lead us to develop a more comprehensive set of responses (as well as analysis and intelligence).

- **Complex**: In the complex domain, the situation is not immediately clear, and there is too much to deal with at once to passively observe. We must first actively probe to get the information required. This quadrant is governed by enabling constraints. There is also no categorization or analysis step, and the response is known as *probe, sense, respond*.

- **Chaotic**: The chaotic domain is truly confusing and can be arrived at quite suddenly. For instance, when conflicting best practices collide to create chaos in the blink of an eye. Often the first thing needed is to *act* to stabilize the situation, then we can *sense* the effect of our previous actions and devise a way to *respond*.

In the middle is the *AC* domain (in the old versions of the framework, this is referred to as the **disordered** domain). **AC** stands for **Aporia/Confusing**. Aporia is a term that in philosophy means *puzzled* or *in the grip of a paradox*. In many cases, it is the best starting point for working with the Cynefin framework, because a case of puzzlement will almost certainly indicate that what we are dealing with does not comfortably fit in the domain of *best* or *good* practice. In this domain, the key question is the type of problem we are facing.

In the AC domain, it is key that we consider the context of the event and develop a view of how the incident is proceeding. To this end, it is sometimes useful to think about the attack in the kill chain framework. The purpose of applying the kill chain model to attacks is to take the situation from disordered to one of the other four. In *Chapter 6, Active Defense*, we will discuss how this works in more detail.

Constraints

Constraints in the Cynefin framework play a specific role. We have already seen one example of constraints in the role played by standards in the coordination game, but the role played by constraints in risky endeavors such as security operations is generally poorly understood.

The types of constraints that are worthwhile to consider in this context are as follows:

- **Governing** versus **enabling**: A *governing* constraint, for instance, a policy, standard, or legal requirement, limits what a team can do. In opposition to a governing constraint, an *enabling* constraint maps a preferred course of action, for instance, in the form of a guideline or best practice.

- **Internal** versus **external**: An *internal* constraint acts like a skeleton that holds an activity together, whereas an *external* constraint defines the outer limits of an activity. A good example of an internal constraint is the team structure during incident response.

- **Connecting** versus **Containing**: A *connecting* constraint acts like an internal skeleton that holds up the framework, whereas a *containing* constraint defines an outer limit.

- **Rigid**, **Flexible**, or **Permeable**: Another quality of constraints is that they can be rigid, flexible, or permeable. A *rigid* constraint is unbending, whereas a *flexible* constraint leaves room for decisions on the spot. A *permeable* constraint is applicable in some places, but not all.

- **Dark**: We can see the effects of *dark* constraints without knowing the cause. A possible example of a dark constraint at work in cybersecurity incident handling is the area or areas *left alone* by the intruders.

Resolving crises

Based on the Cynefin framework, the European Commission and the **Cynefin Centre** published a field guide to managing complexity and chaos in times of crisis, which is, among other things, usable in the resolution of cyber incidents as well.

The field guide is somewhat unusual in that it appeared before the book outlining the complete theoretical framework. It also pays to note that the field guide is *generalist*, and does not specifically deal with cyber incident response, although there is a broad mapping between the contents of the field guide and the incident response loop.

> **Note**
>
> A copy of the field guide is freely available here: `https://publications.jrc.ec.europa.eu/repository/handle/JRC123629`.

The field guide proposes a five-stage approach through which we can achieve the following:

- **Assess**: Assess the type of crisis and initiate a response; determine the type of crisis we're in and work out what boundaries need to be set and maintained.

- **Adapt**: Adapt to the new pace and start building sensing networks to inform decisions.

- **Exapt** or **repurpose**: Exapt or repurpose the existing structures and working methods to generate radical innovation.

- **The pivot** (or [<>]): At this pivoting stage, the story of the incident emerges: what happened, how did it happen, how do all the relevant pieces fit together?

- **Transcend**: Transcend the crisis by rebuilding and recovering.

At each of these stages, the field guide describes some recipes for making sense of the situation, focusing on how to set, manage, and evolve constraints, journaling, documenting the incident, and evolving the incident state until a resolution is obtained. As mentioned before, the crisis guide is a generalist overview aimed at resolving crisis situations in five phases that do not map neatly onto the incident response cycle we discussed in *PART 1* of the book.

The practices discussed in the field guide take us from incident response to *agile* incident response, and ultimately, to active defense. This will be discussed in more detail in *Chapter 6, Active Defense.*

While there is no neat mapping of the stages of the field guide to the stages in incident response, something can be usefully said about which approaches mentioned in the field guide are most useful in the various stages of incident response. *Assess, adapt,* and *exapt* map broadly onto the incident response cycle phases of *discover* and *contain,* and the recipes in these sections form good practices to follow when working in these stages. Similarly, the stages of [<>] and *transcend* map broadly onto the *cleanup* and *recovery* stages of an incident.

Structured analytic techniques

One of the problems analysts face when analyzing cyber incidents is how to make sense of the large quantities of data that are collected during a forensic investigation.

In traditional intelligence circles, **structured analytic techniques** are designed to assist with this process by providing several specific techniques that assist in the process of analyzing large amounts of data, avoiding bias, and generating hypotheses that can be subsequently tested. Especially in long-running, large-scale incidents, teams tend to get in a situation in which the *analyze* portion of the problem can be handled with a structured approach.

Each of the following techniques is a structured approach that has some advantages and disadvantages.

Structured Analytic Techniques

The standard reference for structured analytic techniques is *Structured Analytic Techniques for Intelligence Analysis*, Richards J. Heuer Jr. and *Randolph H. Pherson, SAGE.*

The following list of techniques follows the table of contents of *Structured Analytic Techniques for Intelligence Analysis*:

- **Decomposition** and **Visualization**: This technique is already commonly used in many environments, where complex problems are decomposed into pieces that can be analyzed individually and displayed in a visual way. An example of decomposition and visualization is the use of a timeline for attacks, or ranking, scoring, and prioritizing information.

- **Idea generation**: Idea generation, in the form of structured brainstorming about the observable aspects of an attack and what they might mean, is a key skill for most security teams.

- **Scenarios** and **Indicators**: Scenario development focuses on how a current situation might evolve and on the indicators that will provide early warnings of future events.

- **Hypothesis generation** and **Testing**: This area focuses on cases where the team might have a hypothesis about the incident, for instance, about the initial entry vector, and especially cases where multiple hypotheses are in play. This set of analytic techniques then includes diagnostic reasoning, in which new data is analyzed against the backdrop of all current hypotheses with a view to analyzing competing hypotheses. Other activities in this category include argument mapping, in which all the arguments supporting a hypothesis are rigorously evaluated, and deception detection, in which the possibility that an attacker may deceive us is considered.

- **Assessment of cause and effect**: This is the analysis of cause and effect through the analysis of key assumptions while reasoning with analogies and *outside-in thinking* to analyze the forces that can have an impact on the security posture of an organization.

- **Challenge analysis**: In challenge analysis, we aim to challenge established modes of thinking to broaden the range of explanations or scenarios that are seriously considered during an evaluation. A good example is the well-known what-if question: *What would happen if this or that factor was different?*

- **Decision support**: This area focuses on analyzing the different elements that lead to a decision, for instance, in a pro-con matrix, a **strengths**, **weaknesses**, **opportunities**, and **threats** (**SWOT**) analysis, or impact matrix.

- **Futures thinking**: In futures thinking, we consider a range of possible futures, for instance, in cybercrime, and aim to map out how these futures would impact our decisions and preferences today.

The focus of structured analytic techniques is to promote constructive thinking about incidents and data to turn it into information. It is a good idea to have security teams trained in these ways of thinking and reasoning to improve the quality of decision-making of the team, especially when operating under pressure.

In addition to being useful in incident response, structured analytic techniques can also be used in threat hunting, which we'll discuss more in *Chapter 8, Red, Blue, and Purple Teaming*, as well as threat intelligence, which we'll discuss in more detail in *Chapter 10, Implementing Agile Threat Intelligence*.

Is this part of the security skillset?

A theoretical chapter like this naturally raises questions about how many of these skills security team members should have. In my opinion, members of security teams should be both familiar with Cynefin and trained in the use of structured analytic techniques to optimize their agility in dealing with incidents and empower security operations. This may be a lot to take in. In this chapter, I have only been able to give an introductory outline of what lies in store for security teams that venture into this terrain. Moreover, Cynefin and its related information is often updated, sometimes quite extensively, and knowledge in this area also needs to be kept up to date.

Not every type of incident will be able to benefit from the ideas discussed in this chapter. In general, incidents in the *clear* domain will be automated as much as possible and not require handling by a member of the security operations team as they occur. On the other hand, incidents in the *chaotic* category may not look like incidents at all but may appear as operational issues first.

The *complex* and *complicated* domains involve common incidents that usually do require intervention by the security team as they occur, for instance, spear-phishing, or the initial activities of a **ransomware** gang.

The following figure gives some examples of how incidents fit in with a simplified version of the Cynefin framework, in which the different areas are represented as squares:

Complex

Examples of incidents in this category:

- A server is displaying many quarantined malware instances that appear recent.
- Some of these have low detection rates.
- This server appears to be probing the domain controller with strange kerberos tickets, leading to a large number of events in the logs.

that

Complicated

Examples of incidents in this category:

- An email using the fonts and logos of the business is sent to a small group of senior employees at 4pm on a Friday afternoon.
- The email comes from an IT account and prompts the senior employee to reset their password, otherwise they will lose access to the finance system.
- A link to a password reset page outside of the company domain is provided.

Chaotic

Examples of incidents in this category involve a number of data points in combination, some of which can come from the clear category

- A payroll server is down, impacting the business, with an unknown cause.
- Many logon attempts to the sftp server with common usernames have been observed.
- The sftp server has reported some malware trying to execute.
- Payroll needs to be run tonight.

Clear

Examples of incidents in this category:

- A phishing email comes in, is detected, and put in the phishing queue, showing up in a report the following day. No intervention by the security operations team is required.
- A known piece of malware is detected by the detection and response software and quarantined.
- An sftp server has many logon attempts with common usernames.

Fig 4.4 – Examples of incidents categorized with Cynefin

The key to the ideas discussed in this chapter is captured in the notion that security teams play coordination games within their environments and discoordination games with their adversaries. Especially in the case of an incident, teams are operating in an adversarial environment where mistakes may carry significant consequences and are most often unavoidable. Resolving a cybersecurity crisis is not a game of perfection – it is a game of survival for the organization. The purpose of incident response is to get things as right as possible as soon as possible, but it is futile to hope for more.

Deep critical analytical skills are the core of good security analysis and incident response and resolution. Spending the time to think deeply about how we are operating and why this is so is an activity that will pay large dividends for teams.

Summary

In this chapter, we have discussed some of the basic ideas that underpin thinking about defense and attack, and hopefully dispelled some unhelpful myths. This chapter has only scratched the surface of a large and complex non-technical field.

Specifically, we discussed the idea of cyber defense, coordination and discoordination, a framework for dealing with uncertainty (focusing on Cynefin), structured analytic techniques, and which of these ideas to take on board as a security skillset for members of your team.

In all these activities, the landscape in which we operate has a strong influence on our available options, and the lay of the land in this sense is determined by architecture, and the defensibility of that architecture. That is the topic of *Chapter 5, Defensible Architecture*.

5
Defensible Architecture

One of the five defense approaches is defensible architecture. In this chapter, we'll discuss what defensible architecture is, how it has developed, and how it plays out in several environments. Specifically, this chapter will cover how to design and implement a defensible architecture.

The focus of this chapter is specifically on aspects of the defensible architecture that need to be supported but are often overlooked in reference architectures, such as **resilience**, **survivability**, and **visibility**. The secondary focus of this chapter is on how these characteristics can be designed in architecture.

This chapter will cover the following topics:

- The definition of defensible architecture
- Defense in depth
- The new security boundaries – identity and data
- Roots of trust
- Elements of defensible architecture
- Defensible architecture tradeoffs

We will start this chapter by discussing the definition of defensible architecture.

The definition of defensible architecture

Defensible architecture is about making the design of infrastructure and applications resilient under attack and offers the best opportunities for a successful defense when under attack.

The context of defensible architecture, in terms of the incident response cycle, which we discussed in *Chapter 3*, *Engineering for Incident Response*, and especially in *Figure 3.1* is depicted in the following diagram. This diagram is based on an assessment of current threats and risks, coupled with an in-depth understanding of the business processes and culture. It's aimed at improving cyber defenses, and implementing new applications and infrastructure that have both prevention and detection components to keep out and engage cyber adversaries. Defensible architecture is in turn based on business context, knowledge about past attacks, and threat intelligence:

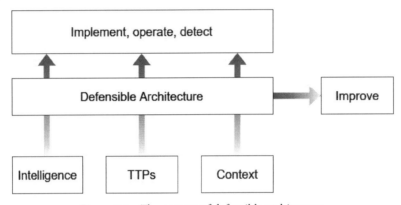

Figure 5.1 – The context of defensible architecture

This definition has a **strategic** and **tactical** component.

The **strategic** component focuses on the types of attacks and threats that the network must be able to successfully defend against. The types of attack that an organization may be subject to depend on its business and the environment it operates in. The success of its defense and recovery depend on its understanding of its own business context and the specifics of the attack. However, attacks will happen, regardless of whether an organization understands the threat landscape or not.

> **A Superior Way to Understand Your Threat Landscape**
>
> A superior way to understand the threat landscape is to use the techniques discussed in the first three chapters of this book and ensure that you capture the incident information of the incidents you have already experienced. Once this is in place, you can go further and consider using cyber threat intelligence.

In addition, the defensible architecture enables **tactical** options when you conduct cyber defense. These tactical options are based on how the network implements those defenses. The key components are **visibility** (or observability) of attacks, and credible options to **contain** and **eradicate** observed attacks.

Pareto optimizable attacks

In many cases, 80% of regularly occurring attacks originate from 20% of adversaries, especially where these adversaries are focused on the specific sector in which the business operates.

> **Note**
>
> As an example, the *silent librarian* group, or the *Mabna institute*, specifically focuses on tertiary institutions (such as universities) with a spear-phishing campaign targeted at obtaining accounts with access to intellectual property. Attacks from this group have been a regular occurrence since 2013. See `https://www.justice.gov/usao-sdny/press-release/file/1045781/download` for the indictment of this group, which also outlines some of their specific methods. These phishing emails were usually highly targeted and believable, and they still are a regular occurrence for cyber defenders in this sector.

This 20% can be described as the persistent attackers. The acronym APT, usually designating a state-sponsored attacker, is also used for some of these long duration groups. Understanding the preferred kill chain of these attackers and mapping them on the ATT&CK framework can pay significant dividends. In particular, it will allow us to design and implement early warning detections for these sort of attacks, making them easier to resolve.

In addition to APT groups, threat intelligence vendors now also classify a FIN group of attackers, which stand for cyber-criminal organizations with primarily financial motives.

Understanding the kill chain

To design defensible architectures, it is helpful to understand the kill chain of the attacker(s) to determine what elements must be implemented to disrupt specific attacks. In the remainder of this book, we will use kill-chain and ATT&CK tactics somewhat interchangeably. To design mitigations against specific tactics, two specific architecture practices are helpful: threat modeling and attack path modeling. These will be discussed toward the end of this chapter.

> **Note**
>
> Specifically, when designing an architecture, consider developing **tactical playbooks** to design the necessary defenses. A tactical playbook is the plan of action for dealing with a specific attacker and attack using the resources that are made available by the environment. Tactical playbooks are not about quickly buying expensive new technology to deal with the latest zero-day attack. We will talk more about tactical playbooks in *Chapter 6, Active Defense*.

The idea of kill chain-driven defense is that for each action taken by attackers, we can consider how such an action could be *detected* and *mitigated*. In what follows, we will base our discussion primarily on the set of **tactics, techniques, and procedures** (**TTPs**) that are collected in the ATT&CK framework.

The definition of tactics, techniques, and procedures in the language of the ATT&CK framework is very specific and it makes sense to define it here:

- **Tactics**: These are the technical objectives of an attacker. They correspond roughly to the steps in the kill chain, such as reconnaissance, persistence, and performing actions on objectives.

- **Techniques**: These are the specifics of how these objectives are achieved. As an example, an attacker may achieve persistence by adding registry run keys to ensure that their software restarts when the machine is restarted. This is one of the many ways to achieve persistence, so, in general, a tactic can have many techniques.

- **Procedures**: These are the specific implementation details of techniques on platforms or with a particular toolset.

The ATT&CK framework is easily available to everyone, is rapidly becoming the standard approach to understanding the details of cyberattacks, and is also loosely modeled on the kill chain, with the tactics in the ATT&CK model corresponding to the steps in the kill chain.

Detection

The intricacies of attack **detection**, apart from being a key element of incident response, is also a key element of the design of defensible networks. Defensible architecture must be capable of determining whether a network, application, or piece of infrastructure is under attack. In addition, *forensic readiness*, especially in the form of a *collection approach*, must be designed in the architecture. We will discuss collection approaches toward the end of this chapter.

Mitigations

In addition to the *detective controls* of visibility and detection, we must also consider *prevention controls*, which make certain adversary actions impossible on our network and hence prevent an attack from proceeding. Some of those prevention controls are architectural. As an example, firewalls will limit the ports as well as the traffic connectivity, and possibly (for a next-generation firewall) be capable of packet inspection and blocking specific packets based on content, which may stop some attack tooling from working correctly on our network.

In kill chain-based mitigations, a common pattern is to consider how adversarial activity may be detected, denied, disrupted, degraded, or deceived.

The idea of how this might work in practice can be considered by following the ATT&CK framework: for each of the tactics and techniques employed by an attacker, we can consider how our defenses might deal with this specific activity of the adversary in our networks in terms of detection, denial, disruption, degradation, or deception. For each technique and procedure, the ATT&CK model enumerates several mitigation options that a defender may employ to thwart that specific activity on their network. The entire collection of mitigations is collected on the mitigations page here: `https://attack.mitre.org/mitigations/enterprise/`.

The discussion in the section *Branches and pivots: how incidents change*, on defenses in the MITRE ATT&CK model, as discussed in *Chapter 2, Incident Response – A Key Capability in Security Operations*, is one example of how defenses may be designed with the kill chain in mind.

Designing defenses based on the pattern of attacks that you already know about may leave important gaps in the defenses. Hence it makes sense to consider a more comprehensive library of known tactics such as ATT&CK. The attack data that's collected in the ATT&CK framework defines a set of mitigations and controls that, when taken together, allow us to map out what we have defended against and what remains to be done in more detail.

Optimal defenses contain both prevention and resilience, as well as components that allow us to detect cyberattacks early. Let's discuss these requirements for defensible architecture in more detail.

Requirements of defensible architecture

At this point, we can define what the requirements are for defensible architecture. The defensible architecture ensures that adversary activity on a network are visible and survivable, and it also ensures that defenders have actionable options. It helps to reconsider the four objectives of incident response, as discussed in *Chapter 1, How Security Operations Are Changing*, and *Chapter 2, Incident Response – A Key Capability in Security Operations*.

Defensible architecture assists with these four objectives primarily through visibility, which assists with minimizing dwell time and understanding motivation and capability. Secondly, defensible architecture is based on measures that make it hard for attackers to perform lateral movement and achieve their objectives, a feature we will call survivability.

Finally, a defensible architecture must enable tactical options for the security team to actively thwart attackers. Tactical options consist of using and repurposing existing tools and capabilities on the network to disable adversaries and stop them before they achieve their objectives, or the introduction of new technical tools and capabilities..

Such tactical options need to be built into the network in advance and need to be designed by the architect. Tactical options can consist of the capability to disconnect endpoints immediately once a compromise is detected, or the ability to immediately deploy additional monitoring. In this sense, security teams need to be agile: able to react to intrusions quickly and fail safely.

This leads us to a set of requirements for defensible architecture. The defensible architecture enables the following:

- **Visibility**: To be able to detect adversarial events. Defensible architectures ensure a sufficient level of telemetry to determine whether an attack is in progress.

- **Survivability**: This is in terms of adversarial actions. Defensible architectures have components that enable the **prevention** of cyber intrusions, but we cannot rely entirely on prevention to stop cyberattacks from being successful.

- **Resiliency** and **redundancy**, which allow the development of tactical options. In general, this means that both the prevention and detection components do not depend on a single point of failure.

In the remainder of this chapter, we will define the specific elements and their configurations that make defensible architecture possible. Before proceeding, however, we will consider defense in depth.

Defense in depth

The traditional pattern for defensible architecture is defense in depth. The main idea of defense in depth is that the defense is not dependent on any single layer. In this sense, the defense in depth architecture differs from (and improves upon) the eggshell architecture, which is based on a hard outer shell and a soft inside.

The basic idea of defense in depth is sound, but there are also some drawbacks. The main problem with the defense in depth model is that it is ideal for an infrastructure that we don't see much of anymore: the on-premises data center. The main two drawbacks of the traditional defense in depth architecture are an implied trust in network segments and trust in endpoints.

Implied trust in network segments

The traditional defense in depth model is heavily dependent on firewalls to segment the network into separate network zones. While there is nothing wrong with a firewall as a preventive tool in defensible architecture, the problem with considering the firewall as the main line of defense is that it may lead to us placing implicit trust into these network segments.

Implicit trust is trust that is not based on an explicit **root of trust**. A root of trust is a specific architectural element that anchors the security posture of infrastructure and is increasingly verifiable.

> **Zero Trust Is Zero Implied Trust**
>
> In recent times, the concept of a zero-trust architecture has become quite popular. The idea of a zero-trust architecture is that no implicit trust is placed in network zones. So, in a zero-trust architecture, for instance, the trust in the office network may be the same as the trust in the public internet: none. Zero-trust architectures rely on verifiable trust in users, assets, and resources. See https://www.nist.gov/publications/zero-trust-architecture for more information. In the context of this chapter, zero-trust architectures may be characterized as zero *implied* trust.

Another risk with the defense in depth approach to security architecture is that defense in depth may become a security bolt-on to a network that has been optimized for ease of deployment.

In the past, it was often common to develop and test applications in flat networks without firewalls, to speed up the development and testing processes. Firewalls were then enabled before deployment, and a ruleset had to be designed at deploy time, with the risk that the ruleset being implemented was over-permissioned to make the application work.

While this model kept networks secure with varying degrees of success, as an example of defensible architecture, it is a failure, since it focuses on implementing security technology on what is possible from a process and technical point of view, rather than from the viewpoint of what is required regarding preventive and detective controls.

Trust in the endpoints of the architecture

Another drawback of the defense in depth model is that it tended to rely on *system hardening* as a preventive measure. System hardening involved a process in which systems and services were progressively disabled while observing the behavior of applications and services that are business critical.

> **System Hardening**
>
> For those old enough to remember it, the early versions of Windows, such as Windows 2000, enabled most services out of the box and had to be explicitly hardened. Fortunately, times have moved on.

Such hardening processes, in turn, enabled an enhanced level of trust in the endpoint, regardless of who was using it or what data was on it. The large risk with this approach to implied trust is that hardening configuration may drift or not take modern attacks into account.

Defense in depth as an evolution

Defense in depth should be seen as an evolution in the development of the defensible architecture that has been useful in many cases, but that, in the time of greater utilization of cloud infrastructures and operational technology, starts to outlive its usefulness.

That is not to say that the elements that defense in depth has required in its security designs, such as system hardening and firewalls, are useless and can now be discarded. They still are, and will remain, important components in **passive defense** and **prevention**.

The approach I'm advocating is that these elements retain their usefulness, but an inclusive view of the architecture, which also considers operations, verifiability of trust, and defensive tactical options as architectural elements, is considered. This is the core of defensive architecture.

If defense in depth represents an older stage in the development of enterprise security architecture that is now slowly becoming obsolete, what is about to replace it? We'll discuss this in the next section.

The new security boundaries

As we have seen, the big vulnerability of the defense in depth model is its reliance on implicit trust in segments of the network or endpoints. The defensible architecture leaves no room for such implicit trust, but instead requires the reasons for trust to be explicit and visible. From the viewpoint of agile security operations, a defensible architecture is composed of the following elements:

- Explicit and verifiable **roots of trust**
- **Visibility** infrastructure
- **Intervention** infrastructure

In addition to these elements, the architecture is based on robust principles that give design guidance in cases where complex technology decisions are required. We will discuss these principles first.

Principles of the defensible architecture

In this section, we will look at three key principles that are the essential ingredients of a modern security architecture. These principles focus on the centrality of identity, the visibility of events, and provable security properties. These principles are examples only, and in your own specific case it is possible that you will use a different set of principles.

Identity

As we will see later in this chapter, **identity** is a key root of trust. Hence, a principle that commits the organization to strong centralized identity and identity life cycle management is a must for a modern security architecture. A principle that captures the importance of identity might read as *Identity is the primary access mechanism to data and code.*

The reason identity is a central element in security architecture is that in modern infrastructure, security is all about being able to tie actions to people. Hence, having a centralized and well-managed identity infrastructure is a key element of security design. With a central identity infrastructure, you can avoid having to manage and monitor multiple identity stores and don't have to start an investigation by trying to tie multiple user names to a single person.

In addition to people's identities, however, we also need to consider *the identities of services* and the *identities of machines*. Infrastructure must include services and machines in the identity infrastructure.

On another note, identity events should be centrally logged and should be searchable with a free-form query. You never know what curve balls will be thrown to the security team during an incident in advance, and smart organizations do not assume the details of investigations before they occur.

Conscientious software

Conscientious software is software that implements telemetry (such as logging) and event monitoring and can maintain a defined security state by implementing robust authentication methods, API security, and code signing. A good conscientious software principle might read as follows:

Software is security-aware, has the right telemetry, and matures toward becoming self-regulating.

With the increasing adoption of the cloud, the execution, and data environment of many of our processes is moving from a network of known and controlled security properties to unknown networks and environments. An increasing number of applications will be consumed as cloud applications. Hence, we require that software that is deployed in the production environment or is a candidate for such a deployment can display either its current capability or has a documented roadmap toward cloud maturity regarding authentication, telemetry, component reuse, the adoption of APIs, and incident response capabilities that allow the security team to address incidents professionally or allow the security team to work together with the cloud vendor toward such a response.

Attestation

An attestation principle might be as follows:

Software and infrastructure can report on their security posture so that a decision can be made to distribute workloads and data to platforms that have the right security posture.

Attestation, using cryptographic verification of integrity and authenticity, should be a near-term requirement for all the architectural elements in a newly designed environment.

With the adoption of cloud, organizations are moving their trust anchors into a distributed environment and hence also moving to a distributed trust model. Attestation provides essential proof of trustworthiness and the means for conducting audits for target computing devices. That is, attestation allows a program or platform to authenticate itself.

Remote attestation is a means for a system to make reliable statements about the pre-launch and launch components in a distributed system. A remote party can then make authorization decisions based on that information. Attestation is an evolving concept and not technically available in the short term for most systems. The next section will be about the roots of trust and how the security properties of data are derived from the roots of trust.

Resilience

When it comes to monitoring, generally, many controls are better than a single control. A resilience of visibility principle might be as follows:

Many points of visibility are preferable over a single point of visibility.

This principle goes back to what we noted in *Chapter 3, Engineering for Incident Response*, in that *many points of visibility are preferable over a single point of visibility*, even if the detection quality of that single point is significantly better than each component of the many points of visibility. The detective capability of many tools working in parallel will quickly outrun any tool standing on its own.

Roots of trust

A root of trust is something that can serve to make us trust something else. More specifically, a root of trust is a set of functions that allow us to imply trust in something that is anchored to a root of trust.

Some roots of trust are verifiable, though most are not (although I'm expecting this will increasingly become the norm). The roots of trust we'll discuss in the following sections are identity, data, and algorithms.

Identity as a root of trust

We have already discussed identity as a central element in the principles driving the security architecture. In addition, identity functions as an important root of trust. Identity functions is a principle because information technology is about people doing things with data and algorithms. An important consequence of this is that we must be able to pin actions to persons.

Identity functions as a root of trust because we trust the person that the identity represents in the role they are functioning in. That may be as an employee, customer, or contractor. To get that right, we need to manage an identity life cycle.

Identity life cycle management is a key aspect of security operations and focuses on the life cycle of our users and the roles they play during that life cycle, as well as how they transition from one role to the next, and the permissions that need to be controlled as part of that transition. Someone may go from being a contractor in May to being an employee in September and being a customer in June. That is one identity in three different roles.

Authentication is a protocol that allows a user to prove to a system that they are who they say they are and how they authenticate to all systems. It is preferable to have a single sign-on system for all applications and maintain the smallest possible number of authentication stores.

There are several reasons for this. First, a smaller number of authentication stores makes it easier to maintain a consistent set of account policies across an organization. Secondly, it helps with detecting events: the use of authentication stores needs to be closely monitored by the security team.

Data controls as a root of trust

Data is not a root of trust itself. The trustiness of data relies on the degree to which data has the properties of confidentiality, integrity, and availability – properties that are usually maintained and proven by something other than the data itself.

The confidentiality, availability, and integrity properties of data are maintained by the following aspects:

- **Encryption**: To avoid inadvertent or malicious disclosure of data, we use encryption. Encryption can also be used as a tool to protect the integrity of data. The use of encryption as a control also leads to the need to store secrets (that is, keys) somewhere securely and control access to them.

- **Secrets management**. The design questions here are about key storage, access to keys and the use of encryption protocols. Secrets management is another root of trust that impacts the security properties of the data that is encrypted with these keys.

- **Authorization**: An authorization control checks whether a user has access to a resource.

- **Configuration**: A configuration control is not a data control but focuses on the device where the data is kept.

- **Data loss prevention** (**DLP**): DLP is a control that focuses on what users can do with data. Examples of DLP controls are limitations on sharing documents in the cloud, prohibitions on emailing documents that are watermarked as *confidential*, and more.

- **Digital rights management** (**DRM**): DRM focuses on who has access to documents and data once it leaves the organization. DRM usually relies on a combination of encryption and key management for sensitive documents and is usually hard to implement and operate.

After going through data controls as a root of trust, let's look at algorithmic integrity as a root of trust.

Algorithmic integrity as a root of trust

Algorithms are what transform data into other data. Increasingly, algorithmic integrity is becoming important as a factor in how we make decisions with big data and AI attacks. AI attacks are a new category of cyberattacks that focuses on subverting the AI algorithm itself.

Algorithmic integrity focuses on whether we can trust our algorithm to work as planned. For most algorithms, this can be verified as a matter of code integrity and functionality testing under varying scenarios. With AI attacks, risks to algorithmic integrity consist of the following:

- **Bias**: Bias can be introduced when and where an attacker influences or modifies the dataset that an algorithm is being trained on. Bias often occurs in AI on its own, when the creators of models do not take a sufficient variety of inputs into account.

- **Input modification**: AI algorithms, at a very abstract level, are black boxes that take inputs (data) and produce outputs (verdicts, decisions, and actions). Because of their black-box nature, it can be hard to relate inputs to outputs, and an attacker who can take control of an input stream can influence the output.

- **Model poisoning**: Model poisoning focuses on the learning stage of AI and aims to subvert the learning of the model to make it produce an output desired by the attacker.

The increased use of AI in applications driving business logic, real-life decision making, and event actions in the real world leads to the need to consider AI infrastructure as a specific element in our overall architecture, as well as the need to develop a risk-based framework that can assess and measure the amount of risk an organization takes on when deploying it.

> **Attacking AI**
>
> See `https://www.belfercenter.org/publication/` `AttackingAI` for a discussion of AI attacks and policy and architecture recommendations on the cyber defense of AI systems. ENISA has also done an initial report on the threat landscape that is confronting AI: `https://` `www.enisa.europa.eu/publications/artificial-` `intelligence-cybersecurity-challenges`.

At the time of writing, there are no widely adopted best practices regarding the security of the algorithmic integrity of AI, but a few recommendations can be made:

- Determine whether AI can be used in a process or whether the difficulty of protecting the AI infrastructure outweighs the benefit of using it.

- Determine whether there is enough data and data of a sufficient variety to train the system.

- Develop a threat model for the AI. For a discussion on threat modeling, see the *Threat modeling* section in this chapter.

In addition to using AI as a tool for business intelligence, it is also increasingly used as a tool in security monitoring. This brings challenges of its own.

AI as a security technology

The second consideration in security architecture is that AI systems are increasingly used as security devices and are subject to the same vulnerabilities mentioned previously.

> **Example – Attacks on AI-Driven Anti-Malware Solutions**
>
> The article *Cylance, I kill you* by Skylight Cyber outlines an attack on the AI-driven Cylance antivirus program by reverse-engineering the AI algorithm and then adding several magic strings to the algorithm that will allow malware to run. It is well worth a read to understand how these attacks differ from usual cyberattacks: `https://skylightcyber.com/2019/07/18/` `cylance-i-kill-you/`.

It is worth considering whether AI brings something radically new to the practice of security monitoring, or, as in the highlighted case, AI is merely used as an alternative way to express signatures, and hence is little more than signature-based security monitoring.

Roots of trust and verifiability

Roots of trust should also be able to be verified. That is, a mechanism must exist whereby we can know that a root of trust is trustworthy and can't be compromised by an attacker. There are two ways of doing this:

- The indirect method uses business processes, logging, and monitoring to verify that the root of trust is trustworthy.

- The direct method uses **attestation**, which we mentioned previously in the *Principles of the defensible architecture* section, to verify that the root of trust is trustworthy.

An example of an indirect method is code signing, which signs executing code with a certificate to certify that it has not been modified between the author of the code and the user of the code. This method is indirect because it transfers the verifiability of the code onto the verifiability of the certificate that was used to sign the code.

> **The Trusting Trust Attack**
>
> A brief paper by Ken Thompson from 1984, *Reflections on Trusting Trust*, makes an argument that you can't trust code that you didn't write yourself in its entirety. This includes the operating system and compiler. A practical example of this attack in operation was the *XcodeGhost* malware on IOS, which involved a malicious compiler for IOS applications: `https://dl.acm.org/doi/10.1145/358198.358210`.

Verifying trust can easily lead to an infinite regress of verifying verification mechanisms. In most practical cases, you must decide which level of verification is good enough to ensure the desired security level. The point is that this may differ for different environments and different systems. The next section deals with some infrastructure elements that are needed for visibility and intervention.

Elements of the defensible architecture

So far, we have discussed security boundaries, as part of the defense in depth discussion, principles, and roots of trust. The defensible architecture also contains several core elements that must be implemented and operated in agile security operations. These elements are a collection of preventive measures, visibility and forensic readiness, and threat-based defenses, which consider threat modeling and attack path modeling. These will be discussed in this section.

Prevention

We have already discussed the set of mitigations that map to the specific techniques and procedures in the ATT&CK matrix, which are collected on the mitigations page of the framework: `https://attack.mitre.org/mitigations/enterprise/`. Such prevention measures are still important components of the security of a system but cannot be relied upon entirely to keep a system secure.

The traditional preventive measures that most people are familiar with are static defenses such as firewalls, signature-based antivirus, and permissions on accounts and filesystems. These are still important configuration items that we must get right.

Increasingly, however, with the emergence of living off the land techniques, preventive security becomes dependent on how a system is operated. In the living off the land approach, attackers use the tools already available on the system to penetrate deeper into the network. The tools that our administrators use to manage the systems are usually permitted to bypass simple static defenses such as firewalls and are not detected by malware detection software. This is because they form part of the normal toolkit that is already present in the system.

Therefore, from an architecture perspective, it is more and more important that we do not only consider the static defenses that need to be put into a system but also consider the operating model: the description of who does what on a system and for what reason. This will ensure that the system tooling has the right access to the system.

In addition, the use of system tooling needs to be monitored and reported, which brings us to the second component of the defensible architecture: forensic readiness.

Visibility and forensic readiness

A key security property of a system is how well you can respond to incidents on it.

Collection approaches are rarely considered in security design. Instead, it is commonly assumed that an assortment of firewalls, antivirus, and logging will be able to take care of defensive needs, alongside a notion of defense in depth. This confuses the relative role of collection and detection and places too much implicit trust in network segments and endpoints, as was discussed before.

One of the key elements of defensible architecture is that it makes decisions about where defenses are put and to what extent they will be employed explicitly. When designing a visibility approach, defensible architecture considers the following:

- **What to collect**: Examples may include event logs, packet captures, specific files, account events such as logon/logoff, process start events, and privilege escalation. It is important to consider this to ensure that, during an incident, we have the correct data. An important pitfall here is that the logging policy on the system itself, which determines what events are logged to begin with, must also be set to the right level.

- **Where to collect it**: Sometimes, especially in the case of packet captures, we have a choice of where to collect them. Event logs are usually collected from endpoints but may involve a log collection server, where logs are temporarily stored and then forwarded to their destination.

- **How to collect it**: This focuses on the technology, such as network monitors, logs, and event collectors, and how to implement and configure them.

- **Where to store the collected data**: Finally, you must consider where and how to store the collected data. The best option is usually a NoSQL database so that data can be investigated with custom queries on the fly.

> **Architecture Pattern – Uncouple Detection from Production**
>
> It is usually a good idea to separate detection infrastructure from production infrastructure. This is because, during an attack, the ability to trust the detection infrastructure is of key importance. An additional reason is that detection and production infrastructure may have different availability and performance requirements. In addition to this, changes to detection infrastructure, which may be required frequently and with high agility, can be made without affecting production infrastructure.

We may not always have a good understanding of the risks and types of attacks that an organization may be facing. In that case, the organization needs a generic approach to collection that has a reasonable chance of determining whether an attack is taking place, but that is also not optimized against a *specific* attack.

An example of what to collect in a generic Windows environment can be found in the ACSC guidance on Windows event logging (`https://www.cyber.gov.au/acsc/view-all-content/publications/windows-event-logging-and-forwarding`).

Architects designing defensible architectures must explicitly consider visibility and detection in the architecture. If this is still vague, it can be made clearer once we consider threat modeling and attack path modeling.

Threat modeling

Threat modeling helps us understand the design aspects of how infrastructure and applications may be attacked, and what can be done to address the risks from attacks in a structured fashion.

Threat modeling is a structured approach to generating threats once the rough application architecture is known. As an example, if you design a house and have a sketch showing a front door and some windows, a threat modeling tool will be able to auto-generate several threats that are associated with having a front door and a couple of windows facing the street, and it will also be able to suggest mitigations (in this case, things such as ensuring that your door and windows are visible from the street).

> **Threat Modeling Tools**
>
> There are several automated threat modeling tools available to assist architects in developing a threat model and documenting it. One of the easiest to use is the Microsoft Threat Modeling tool, which can be downloaded here: `https://aka.ms/threatmodelingtool`. The documentation for this tool can be found at `https://docs.microsoft.com/en-us/azure/security/develop/threat-modeling-tool`.

The threat modeling process depends on what is classified as a threat. A common model of threats is the STRIDE model. Let's look at it in more detail:

- **Spoofing**: Pretending to be something or someone other than yourself.
- **Tampering**: This refers to modifying some data in transit, in storage, or in memory.
- **Repudiation**: This is the process of claiming that you didn't do something or weren't responsible. A repudiated transaction, for instance, is disputed by the originator, which happens, for instance, when you, as an individual, dispute a credit card transaction. Repudiation may be honest or malicious.
- **Information Disclosure**: This refers to breaching the confidentiality of data.

- **Denial of Service**: This refers to abusing or overusing resources, such as computing or network resources, that are needed to provide a service.

- **Elevation of Privilege**: This is a process whereby an attacker, sometimes spoofing a valid user, is allowed to do something they're not normally allowed to do. Examples include a user running code as admin, or a visitor on a website running code on a web server, often due to a configuration or programming error.

An alternative method of classifying threats is to use the library of Tactics, Techniques, and Procedures in a framework such as ATT&CK. ATT&CK also allows architects to design defenses against the techniques and procedures enumerated in the framework, but the result can't easily be captured in a consistent threat model or diagram. A compromise exists to some degree: it is possible to map the techniques and procedures that make up the ATT&CK matrix to the STRIDE model and in this way develop a threat model at a more abstract level.

> The standard reference on threat modeling is: *Threat Modelling; designing for security, Adam Shostack, Wiley*, 2014.

The threat modeling process follows several steps:

- **Diagram**: This involves creating the data flow diagram of an application. A data flow diagram outlines how all the data flows from the user through running code into storage.

- **Identify**: The threat modeling tool provided by Microsoft uses the STRIDE model to automatically generate threats against the data flow diagram. The STRIDE model considers the elements in the data flow diagram and determines which elements of **Spoofing, Tampering, Repudiation, Information Disclosure, Denial of Service, and Elevation of Privilege (STRIDE)** apply to that element and then proceeds to generate threats.

- **Mitigate**: This step details how the generated threats are evaluated, as well as an architectural decision on how they may be mitigated.

- **Validate**: In this step, the architect validates the mitigations.

Threat modeling is a robust way to ensure that threats are considered, but the automated and somewhat abstracted way in which the process works means that just running the threat modeling tool by itself will not guarantee a defensible architecture. Just as important as running the threat modeling tool is to discuss the generated threats, their applicability, and whether corner cases may have been missed. Threat modeling is best used as a starting point for discussion.

Attack path modeling

In addition to threat modeling, it is sometimes useful to model attack paths. An example of attack path modeling is using the *BloodHound* tool to map attack paths through **Active Directory**. Where threat modeling considers the threat to an application or limited piece of infrastructure, attack path modeling considers the compromises of an entire environment by using threat intelligence or detailed threat reports.

So far, we have discussed defensible architecture without referring to the specific environment in which it is supposed to operate. In the next section, we will consider some of the specific tradeoffs that are operating in the three specific environments; that is, on-premises infrastructure, the cloud, and operational technology.

Defensible architecture tradeoffs

As we have seen, defensible architecture is a collection of workflows, practices, strategies, and elements that form a defensible architecture. In this section, we will discuss some specifics of common environments and the tradeoffs that they involve.

On-premises infrastructure

An on-premises security architecture is still often defined by the defense in depth model and characterized by firewalls and implicit trust in network segments. The on-premises infrastructure of data centers are increasingly being migrated to the cloud, and one way to describe what the consequences of that migration are is to characterize it as a migration from an architecture of fear, focused on prevention, to an architecture of trust, focused on trust engineering and visibility.

Migrating to modern architecture is likely to involve the following discussions:

- Trust in endpoints, sometimes called a **zero-trust model**.

- The role and implementation of stronger defenses at the network layer, such as the IEEE **802.1X** standard for wireless networks.

- Enabling office functionality, such as printing, telephony, guest and visitor networks, and presentation and meeting devices such as wall-mounted TVs.

- Internet of Things infrastructure such as **intelligent lighting**.

From the viewpoint of defensible architecture, the key questions about on-premises infrastructure concern the definition and implementation of roots of trust, combining the new security boundaries with the old ones, and how to best implement and maintain a monitoring environment.

Cloud

The cloud architecture is different from the on-premises architecture in almost all these respects and brings in a different set of security concerns and tradeoffs. If we can describe the traditional on-premises data center as an architecture of fear, then the cloud infrastructure becomes an architecture of trust. This is not to say that the cloud infrastructure is inherently better than the on-premises architecture, it is just to point out that the core question of the cloud architecture is one of trust engineering.

The core tradeoffs of the cloud all involve engineering trust:

- When we store data in the cloud, who controls the keys to its decryption?

- How are the identities in the cloud (people, services, and machines) managed and monitored?

- How does code progress from development into production and what are the key steps along the way?

When deploying systems into the cloud, all cloud vendors make good security guidance available to ensure that your architecture is defensible.

Industrial

Industrial networks are the bleeding edge of defensible architecture and are among the most difficult to secure and protect. The well-known **Purdue Enterprise Reference Architecture (PERA)** layers an industrial network into seven layers, again putting implicit trust in network segments that are derived from the presence of security controls at the border.

The main difference in industrial networks is that for the lower layers in the Purdue model, where we have sensors and individual process control, such implicit trust is a requirement, and not something that will be engineered away in any reasonable sort of timeframe. Industrial infrastructures have very long lifetimes, poor security practices at the device level, and impact real processes, in some cases with life-threatening consequences.

That is not to say that the principles of defensible architecture cannot be applied to industrial environments.

The key questions of defensible architecture, which are traceability and visibility, can be implemented in industrial networks, although they require a deep understanding of context. Industrial network protocols differ from the usual IT protocols in that they are used to transport data and settings to industrial devices and contain the values that measure and control industrial processes. Such data makes no sense without comprehending the basics of the industrial process that is being controlled.

Another key element of defensible architecture, threat modeling, and attack path modeling is that it's possible for someone who understands both the technology and the context in which it operates.

> **Industrial Playbooks**
>
> Industrial environments are usually heavily scrutinized for workplace safety, but traditionally, there has been less focus on cyber safety. Industrial environments require a specific set of playbooks, as outlined by Dale Peterson at `https://dale-peterson.com/2021/05/11/3-incident-response-playbooks-for-ot/`.

The discussion on defensible architecture for industrial networks is still ongoing and will be heavily impacted by an increase in high-profile incidents affecting critical infrastructure.

Summary

In this chapter, we have focused on the decisive aspects of defensible architecture, especially the new security properties of identity, data, code, roots of trust, some specific elements of the defensible architecture, and some implementation notes and tradeoffs for various environments.

We contrasted the traditional defense in depth model with the defensible architecture, which is based on explicit roots of trust, the visibility architecture, and the intervention infrastructure. Roots of trust are primarily based on the verifiability of the claims that have been made by them up to a level that, as designers, we consider is enough.

In the next chapter, we will focus on how to operate this architecture by implementing and executing tactical playbooks while considering active defense.

6
Active Defense

In the previous chapter, we discussed defensible architecture and the role static defenses play in the overall security posture. In this chapter, we will focus on active defense practices and how they tie into agile security operations. This chapter will draw together many of the strands from previous chapters and develop an approach to the core of security operations called **active defense**.

Active defense is the practice of intelligence-driven breach detection, containment, and purposed engineering that enables an organization to deal with persistent and advanced attackers. In *Chapter 2, Incident Response – A Key Capability in Security Operations*, we have moreover argued that active defense is intimately connected to the 'inner loop' of the NIST incident response cycle.

You might think that active defense tactics are not necessary for most organizations except in incident response situations. In this view, active defense focuses on deterring persistent and advanced attackers who might not turn up at your doorstep, so you may think that you do not need to engage with this type of defense. To think so is dangerous. Attackers have access to methods and toolsets that would have been considered high-end only a few years ago, and these tools are now used by them to perform intrusions and actions.

Engaging with active defense is a necessity for most organizations. In this chapter, we will cover the following topics:

- The role of active defense

- The agile active defense process

- Understanding the adversary

- Active defense during a crisis

- Active defense for eternal compromise

In this chapter, we will set up an active defense practice based on some of the concepts we discussed in *Chapter 2, Incident Response – A Key Capability in Security Operations*, and *Chapter 4, Key Concepts in Cyber Defense*.

The role of active defense

In *Chapter 2, Incident Response – A Key Capability in Security Operations*, we drew a distinction between an **incident** and a **compromise**, where an incident is something that stops the processes of the business, whereas a compromise is the initial foothold of an attacker.

At this point, we have developed a view on security operations that is based on the notion of ongoing compromise and a generalist view on how to manage and survive crises. Active defense takes this view of security operations into real-life scenarios. Active defense operates during times of incidents and times of compromise but with one big difference: an incident is a crisis, whereas a compromise is business as usual.

If compromise is eternal, active defense is an ongoing activity that involves the security team in a coordinated fashion, with regular assessments, adaptations, turns, and the establishment of a new normal. In this sense, of the five defense types, architecture and passive defense look after themselves, while active defense and threat intelligence require ongoing manual operations in the security team.

We'll outline the approach to active defense later. Active defense practices are influenced by three observations that we have discussed previously in this book:

- The five types of cyber defense, of which active defense is one

- The realization that compromise is eternal

- The realization that incident response is best described as an agile process

By combining these three observations with the approach to incident response that aims to stop attackers from achieving their objectives, as well as limit their lateral movement, we have defined the main idea of active defense.

Active defense as one of the five types of cyber defense

We discussed the five types of cyber defense, of which active defense is one, in *Chapter 1, How Security Operations Are Changing*, and described active defense as focused specifically on **threats** and their *contexts* and how they appear to us. A distinguishing feature of active defense is that it is *proactive* – for instance, active defenders seek out threats through **threat hunting** or intelligence gathering. It also investigates events that match the threat intelligence indicators but were missed by existing controls and detection mechanisms.

> **The Cuckoo's Egg**
>
> The *Cuckoo's Egg: Tracking a Spy Through the Maze of Computer Espionage*, by Clifford Stoll (Doubleday, 1989) is a non-fiction cybersecurity classic and well worth a read. It describes a lengthy investigation undertaken by the author in response to a financial report that would just not add up, although the difference was tiny and attributed to a rounding error by most who looked at it. It was no rounding error. It was a key example of where investigating something *odd* may lead.

As we saw in that chapter, active defense is placed between passive defense and intelligence in the spectrum of types of cyber defense. Like passive defense, it focuses on the defensibility of our organization and interacts with threat intelligence to understand the threat landscape. It also understands the business and its processes to determine where to focus the efforts of the defenders.

Active defense focuses on the following elements of security operations:

- Detecting events based on the development of analytic queries across pools of logging data that take the context of business processes and operations into account.

- Analytically integrating events from host-based, network-based, and artifact-based telemetry.

- Frequently pivoting between these data pools to find additional contextual information to enrich previous events.

- Developing some of those analytic queries into specific security alerts that are loaded onto the SIEM.

- Developing and implementing ad hoc detection and prevention measures that combine business context with live threat intelligence.

Active defense may also include activities focused on the containment and eradication of threats. In this way, active defense pivots between the detect, analyze and contain eradicate and recover in the 'inner loop' in Figure 2.2

First and foremost, active defense is a human activity. Well-organized active *defenders* pick up what passive *defenses* miss. In this sense, active defense is a human activity focused on understanding breaches, along with their context. Active defense builds and maintains context and focus on relevant threats based on a superior understanding of the strengths, weaknesses, and outline of the organization, its processes, and its IT systems. The specific activities that make up active defense are as follows:

- Developing **use cases** and **playbooks**, which we will consider in this chapter.

- Preparing for **active engagement** with an attacker, primarily during the **reconnaissance** and **weaponization** phase of an attack, which we will consider in this chapter. This may also include actions to deny the attacker further access to the network.

- **Threat hunting**, which we will consider as part of blue team operations in *Chapter 8, Red, Blue, and Purple Teaming.*

- **Attack simulations** and **purple teaming**, which we will also discuss in *Chapter 8, Red, Blue, and Purple Teaming.*

In *Chapter 5, Defensible Architecture*, we discussed how such an understanding may be developed at the design stage; in active defense, we can consider implementing these practices in the business-as-usual context.

Compromise is eternal

As we argued in *Chapter 2, Incident Response – A Key Capability in Security Operations*, incident response is the key capability in security operations. The quality of security operations is mainly determined by how well incident response is carried out. We developed the notion of agile security operations by considering the incident response cycle as a human-operated active and agile process and by conceiving incidents as ongoing, rather than on/off events.

Hence, active defense, as the human-operated component of cyber-defense, is a central part of what security teams *do*. What sets active defense apart is its *engagement* with an attack as it is in progress.

The idea of active defense is that, in line with what we discussed in *Chapter 2*, *Incident Response – A Key Capability in Security Operations*, compromise is eternal. Moreover, we treat each compromise as a potential crisis and determine the best approach for handling it. That will require a framework richer than the incident response cycle, which is predicated on the idea that incidents are primarily a break from business as usual and can be resolved with a quick cycle of response.

Agile incident response

In *Chapter 2*, *Incident Response – A Key Capability in Security Operations*, we also set up an agile process for incident response. The agile incident response process focuses on a combination of the incident response cycle and the kill chain. However, active defense, in the light of ongoing compromise, is a set of activities that is more comprehensive than what the incident response cycle will allow.

As it stands, the incident response cycle, which is conceived as a step-by-step process with defined inputs and defined outputs, is relatively static and fits with what the **Cynefin** framework categorizes as *best practice*.

In contrast, the processes that make up active defense do not always neatly fall on a stage of the incident response cycle but draw from a wider context of crisis management. A key realization is that active defense is primarily a human-operated process that deals with threats, threat indicators, business processes, anomalies, and a wide variety of data. In this sense, the active defense process is not so easy to place in terms of best practices. Instead, in this chapter I will argue that active defense can take place on the terms of every quadrant of the Cynefin framework.

To some extent, this is already clear from the *inner loop* of the incident response cycle in the NIST model, which cycles from detection/analysis to containment, eradication, and recovery and back. It is in these cycles that an incident may be transformed from one thing into another. As we mentioned previously, this inner loop is also what makes an incident response process agile.

The key determinant between incident response and active defense is that in the case of incident response, a declared incident exists. Most commonly, in 2021, a declared incident takes the form of ransomware making systems unavailable, which makes it easy to declare the incident; additionally, the fact that an incident is declared means that the context in which detection and analysis will take place, at least initially, is already established.

An approach to active defense

Active defense approaches the problem of eternal compromise through the incident response priorities we discussed in *Chapter 2, Incident Response – A Key Capability in Security Operations*. Active defense engages with the attack and is particularly effective in ensuring that attackers do not achieve their objectives while limiting their lateral movement.

Active defense entails running through some of the steps of the incident response process without having a declared incident. This means that the context of detection and analysis is vague in comparison to a declared incident. Following the framework, we developed in *Chapter 4, Key Concepts in Cyber Defense*, we will focus on using the Cynefin framework to categorize the crisis and develop an active incident response to eternal compromise. Getting this right is the core of agile security operations.

Some of these detections, once a context has been established, may lead to declared incidents. In turn, these may follow the incident response cycle, especially for incidents where attackers have achieved their objectives and managed to create outages and business disruption.

In *Chapter 4, Key Concepts in Cyber Defense*, we discussed the *field guide* to crisis management and suggested that it might be a useful tool for dealing with incident responses for a variety of incidents. In this chapter, this idea will be developed further to create and describe the approach to active defense.

Practices such as those discussed in the *field guide* take us from incident response practices, driven by the incident response cycle, to agile incident response and, eventually, active defense.

In what follows, we will weave these practices into the NIST incident response process to create an approach to active defense that is based on the field guide. It will work during the crisis of an ongoing incident but also be used to steer the ongoing practices of active defense.

The agile active defense process

In our original discussion in *Chapter 2, Incident Response – A Key Capability in Security Operations*, we defined the agile incident response loop as a feedback loop between the **Contain** and **Detect** phases and noted that this inner loop drove the agile aspect of incident response. In *Chapter 3, Engineering for Incident Response*, we considered an expanded incident response-based loop for security operations, which active defense is a part of.

As we pointed out in *Chapter 2, Incident Response – A Key Capability in Security Operations*, the inner loop of the NIST framework is one of the key elements that brings in the agile approach to security operations and active defense. The inner loop outlines the need to frequently pivot between detection, analysis, containment, eradication, and back again to detection and analysis. For the efficiency of incident response, we must understand and manage the cadence of these steps and pivot between them as the situation demands.

Active defense takes this a step further. At a superficial level, in active defense, this inner loop operates even when no alarm has sounded, or an incident is declared. That is, in active defense, we assume compromise and continuously look for evidence of it. What sets active defense apart is that it is a human activity driven by intelligence about attacker behaviors, contextual knowledge about the people, processes, and IT landscape of our organizations, and a strong sense of how attackers may be thwarted using that contextual knowledge.

The following diagram outlines the context of the active defense process in terms of improvements to incident response and security operations. It is derived from *Figure 2.5* and *Figure 3.1*:

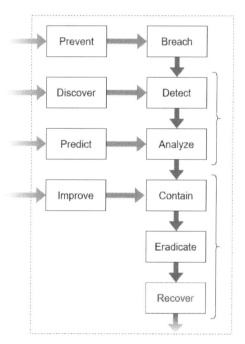

Figure 6.1 – The active defense context in security operations

From this diagram, we can see that the critical success factors for an active defense program focus on the following aspects:

- Preventing breaches beyond using static defenses such as antivirus or firewalls. Active defense needs to deploy specific ad hoc defenses that employ data from threat intelligence or previous breaches.

- Using a toolset that allows one-off detections, such as by developing analytic queries that focus on classes of attacks, alongside a robust store of historical data to mine for patterns and events.

- Accessing threat intelligence to be able to scope out the threat landscape.

- Being able to develop and implement detections and preventions that focus on the early stages of the ATT&CK tactics, especially reconnaissance and weaponization.

To some degree, active defense executes the same steps as incident response. There is, however, a major difference: whereas in incident response a declared incident provides context to the analysis and the subsequent steps of containment, eradication, and recovery, in the case of active defense, there is usually no a declared incident, and the context needs to be established as part of the process itself. Active defense, when done well, can pick up incidents before, or in the early stages of, their development.

In the remainder of this chapter, we will focus on an approach that will allow us to execute these steps against the systematized collection of tactics, techniques, and procedures of the ATT&CK framework, which was introduced in *Chapter 3, Engineering for Incident Response*. In this chapter, ATT&CK will form part of the technology response to compromise and incidents. We will discuss how the ATT&CK framework can be used to define an approach to *threat informed response*.

Devising correct responses and interventions from attacks requires more than just technology. Specifically, it requires a deep contextual understanding of the sector and the business, and a focus on the people and processes of the business.

To bring this component into play, we'll use the *field guide* to crisis management, which we discussed in *Chapter 4, Key Concepts in Cyber Defense*. It is available here: `https://publications.jrc.ec.europa.eu/repository/handle/JRC123629`.

This provides a framework for how we can think of active defense activities. Here, we can look past the constraints imposed by the incident response cycle and build an active defense practice based on a deeper understanding of the organizational context of a crisis.

Understanding and acting on this wider context is important. As we saw when we discussed the Cynefin framework, exclusively focusing on technology leads us to believe too easily that each problem sits somewhere in the category of "can be solved by best practice," and hence is part of the **Clear** quadrant of the Cynefin framework.

In the next section, we will focus on how to use the field guide *proactively*; that is, as a cyber planning and strategy setting tool. This means that we may leave out some aspects of the guide, especially those that extensively deal with non-cyber incidents.

Compromises leave traces that can usually be discovered. Part of the incident response process consists of locating and categorizing the traces of the compromise. During a crisis or an incident, these questions are considered *retrospectively*. During business-as-usual, active defense is about tackling these two questions *proactively* and in a context of people, process, and technology; that is, from the viewpoint of organizational impact. In the next section, we'll focus on active defense as a business-as-usual problem.

Understanding the adversary

Planning for active defense starts with understanding threats and their effects on the business. Specifically, it starts with understanding the **adversary** at a people, process, and technology layer.

People and processes

Understanding adversaries at a people and processes layer is understanding the business model of the attacker – how they make money, how they operate, and, more importantly, where their weaknesses are. Business models are hard to change for most businesses, but the same is true for cyber adversaries.

Several sources for the business model of cyber actors exist.

Arrest warrants of cybercrime gangs make for interesting reading since they reveal a large amount of detail on the organization and the monetization chains of cyber-criminal groups. An example of such an arrest warrant is the one for the *Emotet/Trickbot* gang, which can be found here: `https://www.justice.gov/opa/press-release/file/1401766/download`. As this document makes clear, specific roles exist in cybercrime gangs, such as malware manager (responsible for recruiting and hiring computer programmers, item 52) and malware developer (overseeing the creation of code related to monitoring and tracking authorized users of the Trickbot malware [and] controlling and deploying ransomware, item 57).

Among other things, from this warrant, we can learn that the Trickbot gang engaged in the following activities:

- Transitioning from Dyre to Trickbot

- Acquiring servers, VPNs, and VPS services

- Hiring computer programmers to provide code for the Trickbot malware suite

- Recruiting

- Developing the malware

- Deploying the malware

- Monetizing their activities

What this indicates is a specialized network of operators that work together in a structure not unlike a modern business to develop, distribute, and monetize malware.

The emergence of specific ways of monetizing the proceeds of cyber-crime also led to an increase in **specialization** in the **crime ecosystem**.

This specialization also leads to weaknesses in the criminal ecosystem, which can be exploited by defenders.

Note

A whitepaper that discusses the specialization in the cyber-crime ecosystem, along with possible control points is, *Cybercrime-as-a-Service: Identifying Control Points to Disrupt, Keman Huang, Michael Siegel,* and *Stuart Madnick* (Working Paper CISL# 2017-17, November 2017). The paper can be found here: `http://web.mit.edu/smadnick/www/wp/2017-17.pdf`.

The prevalence of manually operated ransomware gangs, and the research that's been done into their operations, reveals a business model that focuses on specializing in different tactics and using (some of) the techniques in the ATT&CK framework on specific service lines in the criminal ecosystem:

- **Distribution**: This focuses on identifying targets and victims, as well as how malware is distributed.

- **Initial Access Brokerage**: Initial access brokers focus on developing and using exploits or account compromise to facilitate initial access. Expanding remote work options and the increase in the number of people working remotely is leading to easier pickings for initial access brokers.

- **Intrusion**: The intrusion aspect of the malware ecosystem focuses on how the group moves from initial access to complete compromise, where a victim's data is exfiltrated and encrypted.

- **Monetization**: This focuses on facilitating the relationships with the victim and payment, often with cryptocurrencies.

In practice, this distribution of labor means that teams of defenders are up against different departments of the cyber-crime business as an attack unfolds. Each of these will have a *modus operandi* and incentives and criteria for success.

Another interesting consequence is that it is sometimes possible to write specific detections that focus on the **business model** or **tactics** of an attacker. In this context, it is useful to consider the pyramid of pain, which we discussed in *Chapter 3, Engineering for Incident Response.*

As an example, spear phishers fall into the initial access broker category of cyber adversaries because they often on-sell accounts. To successfully on-sell an account, it needs to be tested. Testing usually means logging on as the victim. Such test runs, when performed by attackers, can be detected, and it is hard for adversaries to skip this step while keeping their business intact.

Therefore, detections based on vulnerabilities in the business model are strong predictors of future malicious cyber activity, but they also, in almost all cases, depend on the specific IT context of the organization.

Technology

The ATT&CK framework outlines the details of attacker groups at the technology layer – for example, in the form of the techniques we enumerated under all the tactics we summarized in *Chapter 3, Engineering for Incident Response.*

As an example, under the tactic of **Persistence**, the ATT&CK framework enumerates **Background Intelligent Transfer Service (BITS)** jobs as one of its persistence mechanisms. BITS is used to distribute updates to Microsoft Windows systems but can also be used by malicious attackers to download, execute, or clean up malicious code, as well as for exfiltration.

The use of BITS for malicious activities of this sort is a good example of a living off the land technique, which makes use of functionality already installed in the victim's environment to carry out the adversary's mission.

One of the areas where this structured way of thinking about threats assists defenders takes place is **attribution**. The use of specific techniques may be indicative of the presence of specific adversary groups. As shown in the following screenshot, the ATT&CK framework provides a list of adversaries who have been known to use this technique:

Procedure Examples

ID	Name	Description
G0087	APT39	APT39 has used the BITS protocol to exfiltrate stolen data from a compromised host.[8]
G0096	APT41	APT41 used BITSAdmin to download and install payloads.[9][10]
S0534	Bazar	Bazar has been downloaded via Windows BITS functionality.[11]
S0190	BITSAdmin	BITSAdmin can be used to create BITS Jobs to launch a malicious process.[12]
S0154	Cobalt Strike	Cobalt Strike can download a hosted "beacon" payload using BITSAdmin.[13][14]
S0554	Egregor	Egregor has used BITSadmin to download and execute malicious DLLs.[15]
S0201	JPIN	A JPIN variant downloads the backdoor payload via the BITS service.[16]
G0065	Leviathan	Leviathan has used BITSAdmin to download additional tools.[17]
G0040	Patchwork	Patchwork has used BITS jobs to download malicious payloads.[16]
S0333	UBoatRAT	UBoatRAT takes advantage of the /SetNotifyCmdLine option in BITSAdmin to ensure it stays running on a system to maintain persistence.[7]

Figure 6.2 – The attacker groups using the BITS technique for persistence or exfiltration, as enumerated in the ATT&CK framework (https://attack.mitre.org/techniques/T1197/)

However, attribution is not the most important task for a defender. The additional – and more important – advantage of this categorization is that it allows defenders to determine how such activity may be **detected**, **contained**, and, in some cases, **eradicated**.

An example, also from the BITS technique, is as follows:

Mitigations

ID	Mitigation	Description
M1037	Filter Network Traffic	Modify network and/or host firewall rules, as well as other network controls, to only allow legitimate BITS traffic.
M1028	Operating System Configuration	Consider reducing the default BITS job lifetime in Group Policy or by editing the `JobInactivityTimeout` and `MaxDownloadTime` Registry values in `HKEY_LOCAL_MACHINE\Software\Policies\Microsoft\Windows\BITS`.[2]
M1018	User Account Management	Consider limiting access to the BITS interface to specific users or groups.[6]

Detection

BITS runs as a service and its status can be checked with the Sc query utility (`sc query bits`).[19] Active BITS tasks can be enumerated using the BITSAdmin tool (`bitsadmin /list /allusers /verbose`).[2]

Monitor usage of the BITSAdmin tool (especially the 'Transfer', 'Create', 'AddFile', 'SetNotifyFlags', 'SetNotifyCmdLine', 'SetMinRetryDelay', 'SetCustomHeaders', and 'Resume' command options)[2] Admin logs, PowerShell logs, and the Windows Event log for BITS activity.[20] Also consider investigating more detailed information about jobs by parsing the BITS job database.[4]

Monitor and analyze network activity generated by BITS. BITS jobs use HTTP(S) and SMB for remote connections and are tethered to the creating user and will only function when that user is logged on (this rule applies even if a user attaches the job to a service account).[2]

Figure 6.3 – Mitigations and detections for the BITS technique for persistence, as enumerated in the ATT&CK framework (https://attack.mitre.org/techniques/T1197/)

The ATT&CK framework is a useful tool when conducting active defense and allows defenders to consider the TTPs of an attacker, as well as deploy detections and mitigations against the **techniques**.

In the context of active defense, however, it is better to consider a wider context that also takes threats to the business into account. This means that defenders need to move out of the somewhat restrictive context of tooling and technology and consider the wider impact of threats and crises on the business.

With that preparation out of the way, we can focus on how to create an active defense practice.

Active defense during a crisis

The *field guide* discusses important aspects of how people and processes may evolve during a cyber incident. In this section, we will make some brief notes about the people and process activities that may be particularly useful, in addition to the incident response cycle, in handling a cybersecurity incident.

During a crisis, an organization is unlikely to have the time to calmly sit down and develop a threat model or look at prospective attack vectors.

When the heat is on, it is better to switch to the crisis part of the *field guide* to manage the people and process part of the crisis and use the ATT&CK framework, together with established incident response practices, to manage the technology aspect.

Organizations will be able to use the methods discussed in the *field guide* during an incident as they stand, or as they prove useful.

The following diagram outlines how the field guide works together with the incident response cycle:

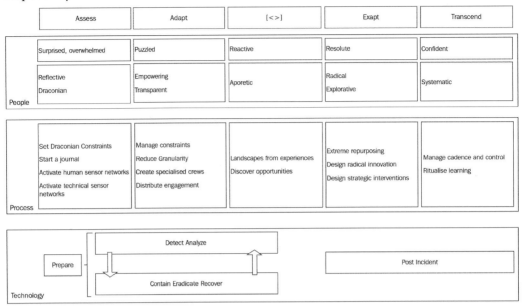

Figure 6.4 – Active defense integrates crisis management with incident response

As we can see, the field guide can be combined with the NIST incident response cycle to add the people and process components to the incident response process, as well as give us an understanding of the operational risks during each phase of the process.

We are at a crucial point here. The active defense cycle takes the practices of incident response into normal operations. This is because we operate on the assumption of eternal compromise. Active defense is assuming the posture of eternal incident response as a normal operation.

Active defense for eternal compromise

Active defense is a set of highly responsive and dynamic practices that have proven their value during incidents but are also necessary during times of compromise; that is, during business as usual. Active defense practices are vital during times of compromise since it is active defense, alongside defensible architecture, that guarantees that adversaries will have a hard time moving laterally and achieving their objectives without being detected and thwarted.

During business as usual, active defense operates even when no incident is declared, meaning that the environment that it takes place in lacks the clarity provided by a crisis.

Instead, active defense activities need to be guided by a robust process that takes the technology, but also the people and processes, into account. In what follows, this process will be structured by following the process in the field guide, weaving insights from ATT&CK into the phases.

The active defense process, during business as usual, assumes that the business is compromised, and the focus is on detecting and evicting adversaries before they achieve their objectives to avoid the consequences of a successful breach. This is not as easy as it sounds since the times from initial compromise to attackers achieving their objectives continue to shrink, and, in the case of some of the more sophisticated ransomware attacks, may be down to mere hours.

Ultimately, though, what that means is that the model where businesses only declare an incident once its effects are abundantly clear is broken. Since attacks are now business-as-usual, something such as active defense, where the core assumption of eternal compromise is met with a set of practices focused on crisis management as a business-as-usual activity, is badly needed.

It is for this reason that the focus of this chapter is to take practices and attitudes from crisis management and put them into a day-to-day set of practices for security operations.

A secondary focus of active defense is to learn from and about the adversary by gathering tools, discovering procedures, and slowing down their tactics. Teams will gain valuable threat intelligence about their attackers in this way.

Assess

In the **assess** phase of the active defense cycle, we map threats to the business and assess what our response might be, should that threat eventuate.

In the field guide, the assess phase typically happens after a crisis has occurred and an organization realizes that they need to expend effort on mapping out the landscape of the new situation they find themselves in.

The assess phase of active defense is different from that since it occurs in either a crisis (incident) or as is the case in what follows (which, as we've discussed, is a state of compromise). We've discussed the use of the field guide in a crisis in the previous section, and here we'll focus on the compromise part.

The two key questions to be answered in the assess phase, according to the field guide, are as follows:

- *Was it possible or plausible* that this event could have happened to us?

- *Do we have contingency plans* in place for this crisis and are we sure we are correctly assessing it?

Using the field guide as a guideline to active defense comes down to apply our knowledge of threats to the business context. To assess the threat level to a business, several sources of information exist. In this section, we'll briefly mention threat models, past incidents, and attack vectors.

Threat models

As part of a cybersecurity strategy, it is a good idea to develop an understanding of threats to a business and a sector. From the viewpoint of the ATT&CK model, a good way to start this process is via the **impacts** tactic and then use this to develop key cyber-attack **scenarios** for consideration.

> **Note**
>
> An example of such a sector-based threat assessment for the maritime infrastructure is the ENISA report on *Port Cybersecurity - Good practices for cybersecurity in the maritime sector*, which is available here: `https://www.enisa.europa.eu/publications/port-cybersecurity-good-practices-for-cybersecurity-in-the-maritime-sector`. This report starts with an impact-based assessment and then works backward.

In *Chapter 5, Defensible Architecture*, we also mentioned threat modeling as part of an architecture practice. Threat models that are developed as part of architecture tend to describe threats to a system level as opposed to an organization level.

In *Chapter 7, How Secure Are You? - Measuring Security Posture*, we will discuss how these threats translate into risk, and how they can be used to measure the overall security posture.

Past compromises and incidents

A good source of information on threats facing the business is past compromises and incidents. From this perspective, it is useful to close the incident loop of past incidents and generate some intelligence on the threats they represented.

When a business has good visibility of its compromises, there is a significant benefit in considering compromises not as individual one-off events, but as being part of a larger story that describes the seriousness, cadence, defense effectiveness, and potential risk of the threat landscape.

> **Example – Email Malware Queues**
>
> As an example, a good method for assessing threats to a business that does not require expensive new tooling is to regularly inspect what is held in the malware queue of the email monitoring system. It is not so much the individual emails that are held but the story told by the collection of emails that is of interest here. As an example, from the list of emails held in the queue, you can determine whether an organization is attacked by common malware gangs such as *Emotet* or *Trickbot*, how often, and when such runs tend to take place. From the origin of these emails, you can also learn a lot about the resilience that the ecosystem of the organization has against such attacks.

A good technique to use when considering past compromises and incidents is to consider the what-if scenario. What would have happened if, for instance, the detection and response software failed to pick up this threat? What is the next line of defense?

Attack vectors

Lastly, an organization can consider the possible attack vectors that exist in its systems. Attack vectors focus on the components of systems that may exhibit vulnerabilities leading to compromises and incidents.

As a non-exhaustive list of attack vector examples, you may consider the following:

- Loss of equipment or theft of equipment
- Credential theft
- Web compromises
- Email compromises
- Use of vulnerabilities and zero-days
- Cloud compromises (such as storage)

This list is not complete, but merely a start of enumerating the many ways in which individual systems may become compromised.

As part of the assess stage of active defense, we have discussed the role of threat models, learning from past compromises and incidents, and analyzing attack vectors. This list can also be viewed as an inventory of threats at an ecosystem and organizational level (threat models), a system level (past compromises), and a component level (attack vectors).

Taken together, this allows an organization to assess the plausibility of incidents and develop playbooks and incident response plans. From the viewpoint of active defense as an ongoing activity in security operations, the most important benefit is that it allows us to develop detections as well as leads for threat hunts.

Adapt

An active defense strategy that focuses on threats that are systematically assessed will focus on what to do about them. This is part of the **adapt** phase. In the adapt phase, a security team will engage with the wider organization to develop playbooks and strategies for dealing with either prospective (in the case of compromise) or real (in the case of incidents) disruption.

In terms of the approach documented in the field guide, this step focuses on developing options and engaging with the wider organization. From a technical perspective, the focus is on developing incident playbooks, exercises, and hunts.

Tactical playbooks

One of the ways to get a handle on how an organization might handle a threat is to develop a **tactical use case**, which outlines an attack vector, and then determine whether our current defenses and incident response processes would be up to the task.

> **Use Cases and Playbooks**
>
> In what follows, it makes sense to distinguish between a use case and a playbook. A use case is an attack scenario, usually characterized in terms of ATT&CK TTPs, while a playbook is the sequence of steps that are followed by the security team during incident response.

When developing a use case, we can take the scenarios developed in the assess phase and develop and document an organization-wide response to that use case and collect our responses to it in a playbook.

The advantage of use cases is that they allow an organization to consider key questions about processes, decision making, documenting, and communication. Some examples of questions that can be asked in use cases that form useful parts of incident response planning and playbook development are as follows:

- At which point are systems turned off and who has the authority to make that decision?
- Who is in charge if the main responder is not available?
- Can you restore from a backup?

Playbooks can be created and managed with modern tools such as wikis and planners. With these tools, playbooks can be made highly engaging and interactive.

A particularly important part of the response cycle that needs to be considered is **recovery**. Recovery is often left out of specific incident response plans, apart from the side note that it needs to happen but is rarely considered and exercised as part of active defense. Yet the speed with which a business can recover from a cyber-attack is a key determinant of how well the business can respond to adversaries.

In *Chapter 2, Incident Response - A Key Capability in Security Operations*, we outlined a team structure that consisted of operations, planning, and communications. For complex and large infrastructures, it may be a good idea to separate incident planning from recovery planning and have two people executing these roles while working in close cooperation.

Some key questions to consider in recovery planning are as follows:

- Where are the backups of this system kept?
- What credentials are used to access backups? Are they identical to the ones used by the system administrator?
- How long does it take to recover data from a backup?
- How much data will be lost when a system is restored from a backup?
- Who will be required to assist with system recovery for this system?

Let's now discuss incident response exercises.

Exercises

While playbooks are exercises in documentation, **incident response exercises** (sometimes also called **dry runs** or **Table Top Exercises** (**TTX**)) take the concept one step further. In an exercise, we take the team through a simulated incident to ensure that the processes that we have developed work in practice.

Exercises allow organizations to iteratively become better at managing incidents and practice incident response at an organizational level.

Planning and executing exercises is time-consuming but rewarding. Some of the advantages of conducting exercises are as follows:

- They allow the organization to devise possible scenarios for cyber-attacks on the organization. This can, for instance, be based on a what-if scenario using some of the available compromise data, or it could be a scenario that has happened to a competitor and about which information is available in the public domain.

- Exercises do not need to stop at a single organization. They can also involve multiple organizations that work together in an ecosystem.

- They allow an organization to play out how a scenario would unfold in practice.

More information on conducting cyber exercises, including collateral and a handbook to get started, can be found here: `https://www.cisa.gov/cybersecurity-training-exercises`.

Hunts

Threat hunts take this process one step further. In a threat hunt, the team uses the information and data sources already established and goes out to discover evidence of these threats on the network.

In many ways, the adapt phase forms the core of some active defense practices that we will discuss in more depth in *Chapter 8, Red, Blue, and Purple Teaming*.

The pivot or [<>]

This phase may or may not occur during active defense. The [<>] stage is where a team has not been able to make sense of all the findings from activities in the assess and adapt phases and is still trying to piece the puzzle together. In this sense, the [<>] phase is a diagnostic phase that is key to transforming the security operation into a new normal, in which an expanded range of threats can be detected and mitigated.

Define sources of visibility

Several problems may lead to the puzzlement that characterizes this phase. The first is that a team may lack the right data sources.

> **Battle for the Logs**
>
> In my experience, setting up a new defense capability always starts with a battle for logs. In many cases, organizations do not have a robust logging and collection strategy unless cyber security demands it.

One of the reasons that teams may not be clear about whether they have all the data they need is that the organization lacks a **logging strategy**. In *Chapter 5, Defensible Architecture*, we discussed the practice of collecting data for newly designed infrastructure and applications, but that does not help with already existing infrastructure where such elements need to be engineered onto existing applications and infrastructure.

Developing use cases, which we discussed previously, will assist with developing a logging strategy. A use case follows a specific scenario step by step and allows defenders to consider what log files they would need to be able to detect that activity, as well as the analytic queries on those log files that would surface those events.

Establish context

Another problem that comes with not having enough data is lacking the context of the existing data.

> **Artificial Intelligence**
>
> A common problem security teams think they have is that there is too much data and too little time to make sense of it. **Artificial intelligence** can be used as a tool to remediate this problem. In practice, I would suggest that, in almost all cases, teams should approach this problem from the perspective of a lack of context first. This means that the problem is not one of having too much data, *per se*, but one of having a lack of understanding of what the data means. This also means that teams will struggle to distinguish between meaningful, useful data and data that does little to advance the cause of defense. Badly implemented artificial intelligence solutions tend to exacerbate this problem by just expanding the alert stream.

There is no substitute for deep insight into the business itself when it comes to establishing context.

Exapt

In the **exapt** phase, the new normal is built. This is the phase of emerging the structure. In this phase, a team may focus on tactical optimization or pareto optimization, or new tooling. In the exapt phase, in a broad sense, a new order emerges after a crisis, and in the context of active defense for eternal compromise, the exapt phase describes a stage where things move from active defense to passive defense by becoming standard detections and **standard operating procedures**.

In other words, the exapt phase describes a process that teams can use to move from dynamic activities such as threat hunting, exercising, and developing the threat landscape for their organizations, to embedding responses into an established framework of passive defenses.

In many ways, this phase is critical in being able to *realize the value* of the more dynamic active defense activities.

Tactical optimization

Tactical optimization focuses on optimally deploying already existing toolsets. A common problem in cybersecurity is that organizations fail to fully implement the tools they already have and leave detections and mitigations unconfigured or turned off, often in the mistaken fear of breaking something on the network, or due to lack of time and focus.

> **No New Tools**
>
> I sometimes have a *no new tools for the next 6 months* approach to give teams time to fully configure the tools already there. This is often one of the most cost-effective ways of upgrading defenses: no new license fees, no new deployments – only making changes to what is already there. Teams should also focus on having a robust security engineering capability to ensure they get the most out of their current investment.

A good approach at this point is to pay close attention to the implementation, detection quality, and prevention quality of the existing toolset by using the stream of generated alerts as a guide. The process of **detection engineering** focuses on achieving this objective.

Pareto optimization

As we mentioned previously, in *Chapter 5, Defensible Architecture*, attacks are pareto optimizable. This means that most attacks are usually of a similar type (phishing, malicious office documents, email attacks, and scanning, for example). This is an advantage for security teams, in the sense that effective defenses against these common types of attack will pay outsized dividends.

It is a good strategy if you seek to automate (or optimize, if the process must be manual) the detection and response to these attacks to free up time for the security team to focus on the minority of attacks that do not follow the common pattern.

In the exapt phase, such automation practices and compromise playbooks are established.

New tooling

In some cases, a team may decide that critical gaps in defenses exist, and that new tooling is required. In this case, the ATT&CK framework provides good guidance on where the gaps exist and where new tooling may help.

When tooling decisions are made from this perspective, it transforms the dynamic of sales calls, putting the power of fear, uncertainty, and doubt back where it belongs: with the customer.

Transcend

In this phase, the new normal is established, and what's been learned from compromises (as well as incidents) is incorporated into best practices and codified processes and procedures.

Pareto optimization

In this stage, the team changes to a new state, where some of the work that was done in developing playbooks, hunts, and integrations has led to permanent changes in operations. This may be as simple as a new set of dashboards to monitor, better and more reliable detections, or changes in how compromises are tracked and reported.

Bottom-up strategy

You may have noticed that implementing a robust set of active defense approaches that takes the people and process components into account amounts to a bottom-up strategy for cyber-defense. We will have more to say about strategy in the next chapter.

Summary

In this chapter, we discussed active defense from the viewpoint of integrating people, processes, and technology. Active defense must be an all-organization effort and not something that's done just by security teams.

The technology component we focused on was the inner loop of the NIST incident response framework. The important takeaway from this is that active defense may operate components of the incident response cycle with or without an incident being declared, as part of our compromise is eternal approach to cybersecurity.

In this chapter, we widened the scope of incident response to encompass active defense and defined a foundation for active defense practices based on the guidance in the field guide. Among these active defense practices is threat hunting, threat modeling, and others.

The field guide also prompts us to focus on the social and organizational aspects of active defense.

For the people and processes, this includes incident response. Using some of the tools from the field guide for crisis management is a useful way to learn how active defense operates.

As we have seen, these processes operate during actual incidents but also during the *business-as-usual* phase of active defense, which is characterized by compromise.

In the next chapter, we will focus on how these practices integrate into a cyber program by looking at risk management and reporting.

7
How Secure Are You? – Measuring Security Posture

In this chapter, we will talk about security posture. Security posture is a measurement of how ready you are to deal with a cyber-attack. The security posture is set during the development of the security strategy. Not surprisingly, the security posture is complex to measure, hard to maintain, and closely related to the value that a robust security operation brings to the business.

Traditionally, discussions about security posture have focused on reducing risk, rather than driving business value. This chapter will focus on how practitioners should have these discussions in the context of business value.

In this chapter, we'll focus on risk assessment, the security posture, the security strategy, and how security is crucial for a business. Specifically, we'll cover the following topics:

- Security as risk reduction
- Measuring risk reduction
- Strategy maps – security as business value
- Working with the security strategy map

The focus of this chapter is to discuss how risk management and strategy definition can be impacted by the agile security operations concepts that are discussed in this book.

In terms of the agile security operations loop, the approach in this chapter primarily interacts with the **recovery** and **retrospective** aspects of incident response. In other words, this chapter considers risks, reviews, and how they feed into the security posture and its strategy.

Security as risk reduction

The strategic goal of cybersecurity is two-fold: reducing risk to the business and enabling new business initiatives. We'll discuss risk reduction first.

In *Chapter 1, How Security Operations Are Changing*, we discussed the risk-based approach to security and how the overall residual risk to assets is based on the exposure, the level of vulnerability, and the available controls, as described in the NIST risk management framework here: `https://csrc.nist.gov/publications/detail/sp/800-30/rev-1/final`.

A framework for risk reduction was depicted in *Figure 1.1*, in *Chapter 1, How Security Operations Are Changing*. This figure has been reproduced here, also indicating how the various areas map to various areas of the ATT&CK framework, which we will use to develop our discussion of risk:

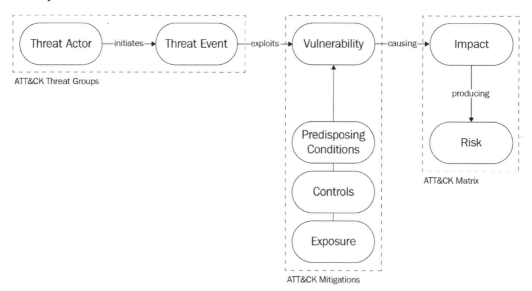

Figure 7.1 – Risk model from NIST 800 30r1 using the categories of the ATT&CK framework

We will discuss the management and treatment of risk in more detail shortly, through an approach based on the ATT&CK framework, which we used earlier in this book. This framework is particularly helpful in answering those questions.

The factors that play a role in this risk framework are as follows:

- **Threats**: Threats have threat actors who execute threat events. Threat actors are typically threat groups who run campaigns or targeted intrusions. In terms of the ATT&CK framework, threats are composed of threat actors and threat events, and threat actors are indexed in the framework.

- **Exposure**: Exposure can be managed by minimizing the attack surface, such as not opening unnecessary ports on the firewall, disabling any services that are not needed, or limiting the types of networks allowed to connect to a service.

- **Vulnerability**: Vulnerabilities exist all the time and are the result of either programming errors in our own or someone else's code, or configuration errors.

- **Controls**: Controls were described in *Chapter 5, Defensible Architecture*, in terms of roots of trust and visibility of events.

- **Impact**: The ATT&CK framework describes the impact of the techniques that adversaries use to disrupt availability or compromise integrity by manipulating business and operational processes (`https://attack.mitre.org/tactics/TA0040/`).

From this, we can determine what the key questions are for risk management in organizations.

It all comes down to a combination of impact and controls. Controls usually take the form of static defenses that block certain routes, from threat events to impact. Controls focus on threat reduction, as well as limiting exposure or a vulnerability, by severing the link between the threat actor and its impact. In terms of the five types of cyber defense, the implementation and operation of cybersecurity controls are primarily what we do as part of **passive** defense.

Impact determines the amount of loss an organization may suffer if the risk event occurs. In terms of this risk framework, minimizing the impact is also desirable, and this is what we aim to do in **active** defense, as discussed in *Chapter 6, Active Defense*. Defending actively is about having the resilience and response capabilities to ensure that the impact of the risk is minimized.

As an example, an attacker that has established command and control on our network and is trying to pivot to a more privileged point (an account, device, or service) on the network has already caused an impact. Their objective is to get more impact. The aim of active defense at this point is to limit the impact that the attacker has already achieved. From the viewpoint of the attacker, this is not enough. This realization is the background behind our earlier statement, in *Chapter 1, How Security Operations are Changing*, and *Chapter 2, Incidence Response – A Key Capability in Security Operations*, that defense aims to detect and contain attackers before they have reached their objective.

Cyber defense, which engages both active and passive defense, must consider risk from the following perspectives:

- The description of the risk. It is important to have an accurate understanding of what the risks that we are trying to manage are.

- A *qualitative* understanding of the risk by focusing on the impact that would occur if the risk materialized.

- How to translate the risk into a meaningful *quantity* that can be used in financial planning?

- What controls are available to manage the risk?

- Which of the available controls is the best for managing that risk?

Usually, it is not possible to fully control risk, and a certain amount of residual risk remains after all the controls have been applied. Residual risk is the risk that remains once controls and mitigations have been applied. We will understand residual risk better once we measure risk reduction.

Measuring risk reduction

In *Chapter 1, How Security Operations Are Changing*, we discussed a risk management framework but also noted that a risk-based approach to security runs the risk (pun intended) of overfocusing on passive defenses – that is, controls that can be implemented once and left alone.

As we stressed in *Chapter 1, How Security Operations Are Changing*, security operations are about more than just passive defenses; they focus on the activities that are performed during security operations that help promote resilience. In this section, we'll discuss how we need to rethink risk to take that into account.

The key to getting to an improved risk management framework is to have a reliable set of metrics that measure the **resilience** of an organization against cyber-attacks. This includes the measures an organization takes operationally to mitigate the impact of realized risks – that is, risks that have occurred – as well as how an organization assesses and implements risk management for future lines of business.

A robust framework for the management of risk has been developed by NIST (`https://csrc.nist.gov/Projects/risk-management`) and is documented in the NIST 800-30r1 document (`https://csrc.nist.gov/publications/detail/sp/800-30/rev-1/final`). This document is quite comprehensive and discusses the risk management framework in detail.

Description

To understand risk, it is necessary to describe it. The ATT&CK framework helps describe risks emerging from cyber events. There are several ways in which the ATT&CK framework assists in describing risk:

- **Threat groups**: As is apparent from *Figure 7.1*, risks start with threat group actors and threat group events, and the ATT&CK framework contains a list of groups and associated tactics and techniques.

- **Mitigations:** Another handle on risk is to consider mitigations that have not been applied to the environment, which correspond to existing unmitigated vulnerabilities.

- **Impact:** The third approach is to focus on impact.

> **Note**
> These three approaches are discussed in NIST 800-30r1 on page 15 of the document.

A useful source of information to inform risk descriptions is to focus on past attacks and assume a scenario in which one or two controls that worked in the past, have now failed.

A practical example is malware-laden emails that are being stopped at the border. Few organizations look at this in detail, but by not inspecting this type of information, they are missing out on something. The collection of emails that are being held tells a story about actors that are consistently trying to enter our environment (and up to now, have kept failing). What if, one day, they slightly improve their malware and succeed?

Understanding the cadence of these events is interesting too. As a further example, the *Emotet group* (largely arrested in January 2021) tended to attack in phases with different iterations of the malware (sometimes referred to as **epochs**). This sort of activity is easy to spot by inspecting malware queues at the border, and evidence of a large amount of malware being held should lead to increased vigilance inside the network.

Don't confuse the risks themselves with tactics, techniques, or their impact. The impact is a component of the risk framework that is primarily responsible for the financial losses associated with risk, as discussed in the next section; it is not a description of the risk itself. Suffering the impact is part of the description of the risk.

A risk heat map may be developed if we consider the combination of threat groups and mitigations, outlining where the organization is at most risk. Usually, the heat map maps the identified risks on a scale of likelihood/impact.

Financial aspects of risks

Using heat maps is one way to model risk, but a heatmap can be hard to contextualize into a business context. Having a list of risks labeled red, amber, or white, along with some risk descriptions, does not give an organization good guidance on how to treat these risks and gives only a hazy understanding of the potential impact of these risks on the financial bottom- line.

To understand the meaning of a risk to the business, it needs to be understood in financial terms. To understand the financial impact of a risk, it is necessary to understand its business impact and technical impact first.

Technical impact starts with systems and can be related to the impact column in the ATT&CK framework. This may be loss of data, exfiltration of confidential or private information, destruction of systems (and equipment in extreme cases involving control systems), or hijacking resources, leaving the cost of their use to the business.

The business impact is described in terms of the direct costs that occur when a system is hijacked, or the costs incurred when a process stops working, the reputation lost, or the revenue that's not earned if a system is unavailable.

> **Measurement in Cybersecurity**
>
> A useful set of recipes and approaches to translating the traditional risk approach into business terms can be found in - *How To Measure Anything in Cybersecurity Risk, Douglas W. Hubbard* and *Richard Seiersen, Wiley,* 2016. The tools discussed in this book, as well as more information on this approach, are available on the associated website: `https://www.howtomeasureanything.com/cybersecurity/`.

To approach risk from the business impact end, a sound understanding of process and systems architecture, as well as a threat model, is a good starting point. This type of information enables an organization to perform an impact analysis, which outlines, in business and process terms, what would fail if a certain risk occurred.

How to understand and describe these models was discussed in *Chapter 5, Defensible Architecture.*

Controls

The next two subsections focus on controls – both the controls that are available to manage risk and selecting the best controls to manage the risk. Cybersecurity controls that may be used in risk management are cataloged in the NIST 800-53 series. This is a base catalog of controls called a **control baseline**. From this baseline, organizations may select a subset of controls that are relevant to them. This is called an **overlay**.

The 800-53 control baseline is best viewed as a collection of possible controls, but not something that needs to be implemented in its entirety. Specifically, it will need modification, interpretation, and specific operationalization to fit in with the environment that it will be applied to.

The NIST control set works with a collection of overlays that assist organizations in defining the control set based on the scenario they face. As an example, the **industrial control system (ICS)** overlay provides a recommendation for the controls to implement in this scenario. The things that an overlay will specify are, usually, the following:

- Controls that need to be deleted, added to, or modified from the baseline.
- Technology-dependent applicability and interpretations of controls.
- Specification of certain acceptable values for the control.

In this way, control overlays can manage which controls are implemented and how they are implemented, and they can contain any amount of specific technical detail referring to a system, even down to specific acceptable values for certain controls.

NIST maintains a comprehensive website on risk management (`https://csrc.nist.gov/projects/risk-management`) that focuses on control selection for certain scenarios.

Controls and policies may look like quite static, non-agile ways of running security operations. Nevertheless, they are essential for communication with the business, as well as managing the passive elements of security.

Control frameworks and risk management may also drive aspects of a more active mode of defense, where defenders specifically seek out and interrogate violations of policies, un-monitored controls, or control violations. This is often useful for several reasons:

- It assists security operations significantly with gaining and understanding the context in which the business operates, as well as outlining some future rabbit holes that attackers may attempt to slip through. All in all, this sort of work helps with understanding the map of possible attack paths through the business.

- Highlighting and measuring gaps in controls and modifying the control overlay in use by the business.

- Deriving additional controls and monitoring points based on the analysis of the attack path.

In addition, it is also useful to consider the ATT&CK mitigations in the context of a control framework to determine the sort of attacks that the adopted control framework is capable of preventing, monitoring and resolving.

Risk management versus enabling the business

There is more to risk than just reducing already existing risks. The security author Derek Brink calls these **already existing risks**. Unrewarded risks are risks that exist in the business as it is today and taking these risks does not add to new revenue or improvements in revenue.

You can also think about risk management in terms of **rewarded risks** – calculated risk-taking to support the new opportunities that can be created once security is done right.

This leads us to a brief excursion on security strategy, which is the subject of the next section.

Strategy maps – security as business value

It is a somewhat stale statement that security should contribute to the business to enable new business initiatives. You might also say this by stating that security should be an enabler of the business, rather than a blocker. Yet this is easier said than done – it is hard to determine how security enables the business.

To map out how an activity contributes to the wider goal of an organization, especially in cases where conflicting activities and goals need to be balanced, a compromise created, or a new innovative solution found, businesses need to develop a **strategy**.

Strategy is a commonly misunderstood term. A strategy is not a plan. A strategy is what you need when you're dealing with a situation in which outcomes can be uncertain based on the actions of others. A good strategy considers scenarios and is grounded in a deep understanding of the drivers of business processes, value chains, and how attacks compromise these chains.

> **The History of Strategy**
>
> As Lawrence Freedman argues in his *Strategy, A History* (*Oxford University Press*, 2014), strategy only became separated from tactics once the size of the armies necessary to wage war had grown to such a size that a separate staff department was required to manage the logistics and planning for an army of that size. The term then made it from warfare to business.

Strategy is about how an organization aims to reach its goals in an environment where the actions of other players in that environment are uncertain, multiple future scenarios might be possible, and the organization has objectives that are, at times, in conflict. It is because of this that strategy is not a plan. Not everything is under control.

This somewhat uncertain nature of strategy development leads to a widespread mystification of what the strategy process entails, which leads to many organizations getting the strategy wrong. The common pitfalls that hamper mature strategy discussions in many organizations are as follows:

- Having strategy discussions without the corresponding visibility of the environment
- Not modeling risk properly
- Not understanding the business context properly

All in all, risk management, as discussed in the previous section, is key to the development of a sound security strategy. As we have seen, to perform risk calculations properly, a significant amount of visibility is required to assess the operation of a control framework, and the approach of assuming scenarios in which current controls fail is a useful way to assess the impact of cyber threats to the business based on real attack data.

Risk modeling and business context are the two key areas where insights gleaned from security operations have considerable strategic impact. To avoid the common pitfalls of strategy development, it is necessary to have visibility into the environment and a risk framework.

> **Strategy Maps**
>
> To capture how strategy contributes to organizations, in 2001, Robert Kaplan and David Norton expanded their model of the balanced scorecard to **strategy maps** in their book *The Strategy-Focused Organization* (*The Strategy-Focused Organization: How Balanced Scorecard Companies Thrive in the New Business Environment*, Boston, MA: *Harvard Business School Press*, 2000).

The tool that we will use to discuss matters of security strategy is the **strategy map**, which is an evolution of the balanced scorecard.

Constructing strategy maps

As we discussed in the previous section, creating, and setting up a strategy is not a simple matter. Strategy is not a plan, but rather the definition of a specific focus or set of responses to imaginable scenarios.

As an example, the four goals of incident response, as discussed in *Chapter 1, How Security Operations Are Changing*, form a strategy for dealing with incidents, so, they are a good starting point for agile security operations.

The complexity of strategy is not the entire story, however. Strategy focuses on three specific aspects of the business, which roughly translate to the why, the what, and the how of the business, which are as follows:

- **Value creation**: Why is the business there at all?
- **Business processes**: What processes underpin the process of value creation?
- **Capabilities**: How are these processes operated and are there specific gaps that need to be filled?

In addition, a strategy also considers how all these elements are aligned.

Strategy map layers

The strategy map has several layers, indicating that it looks at the totality of a business from multiple points of view. These layers are as follows:

- Financial or value
- Customer
- Operations
- Capabilities or learning and growth

In the strategy map, the discussion of value creation, processes, and capabilities is focused on these four layers: financial, customer (both representing value creation), operations (representing the business process focus), and capabilities (representing the how).

For a cybersecurity strategy, value, processes, and capability are similarly relevant. The four goals of incident response form the why of security operations. The what is covered in the five types of cyber defense and the processes that make up security operations, while the how is covered in the capabilities that deliver it all. The latter will be discussed in more detail in *Chapter 9, Running and Operating Security Services.*

Security strategy maps

Is a strategy map for a security strategy possible? The answer to this question relies on whether we can capture the value of a security program in terms of financial, customer, operations, and capabilities metrics. We are generally not used to discussing the value of a security program in financial terms or customer perspectives. As security practitioners, we are generally pretty good at discussing the operations or capabilities of a program. Hence, developing a strategy that works from a business perspective has traditionally been somewhat of a challenge.

> **Strategy Maps for Security**
>
> A series of articles by Derek Brink on the `securityintelligence.com` website contains a development path for a security-based strategy map that follows the Kaplan and Norton model. See `https://securityintelligence.com/a-strategy-map-for-security-leaders-applying-the-balanced-scorecard-framework-to-information-security/` for the start of the series. This forms a good starting point to start thinking about a strategy for security.

In terms of agile security operations, a strategy may be articulated as a set of agile principles, practices, and benefits that are typical of agility in security operations, in addition to the strategy that already exists.

At a high level, we may capture the development of a security strategy with the strategy map in the following terms:

- The financial or value of agile security operations should be expressed in terms of the improved defensibility of the business, expressed in terms of either risk buydown or new initiatives that can be enabled once security is in place.

- The customer perspective can be captured in terms of more rapid recovery after an incident, or a reduction in the need to perform incident response at all, since incidents are caught earlier and with better fidelity.

- The operations perspective can be augmented with the set of practices we discussed in *Chapter 6, Active Defense*.

- Capabilities or learning and growth focus on how we learn from past incidents, as well as the specific practices and incidents gained with agile security operations.

This is a good starting point for organizations that already have a security strategy and are looking for specific points of view emerging from agile security operation to augment how they articulate and communicate strategy.

But what about organizations that must start from scratch and have nothing at all? The following section contains a few useful pointers.

Starting a security strategy

For organizations at the beginning of the security journey, it can be hard to determine how to start. This section outlines some high-level steps that can be used to start work on a security strategy:

1. Get some visibility of the current environment and the elements that are currently in place.

> **Note**
>
> Most organizations have firewalls, for instance. Are the firewall logs available to get some more information on what is currently happening? What is currently allowed or blocked by the firewalls that looks like malicious activity?

2. Use this information to understand and map the threats to business processes using the scenario planning method mentioned previously. Focus on what happens if a control or measure fails.

3. Translate those threats into risks and prioritize the risks.

4. Understand and map the necessary controls to counter those threats using, for instance, ATT&CK.

5. Develop a plan of action to implement those controls.

This is a bootstrapping method of the security strategy that uses already existing information, together with some imagination and the work that's already been done in developing the ATT&CK framework, to develop an improvement plan.

With these improvements, the visibility into the environment will also increase, leading to a virtuous cycle of improvement in the security posture.

Now that we have defined the outline of a strategy map, we'll consider how to work with them, and what they mean in practice for a security program.

Working with the security strategy map

Another way to capture the benefits of a strategy is to have a value map. This maps out how valuable an initiative – in our case, agile security operations – is to an organization, as well as how effective the proposed principles are.

In this section, I will outline a few metrics that organizations can use to map the effectiveness of their strategy onto a set of metrics in terms of financial measures, customer measures, operations, and capabilities. The latter focuses on the effectiveness of security operations and indicates the means of improvement.

Financial metrics

The financial metrics of the security strategy are primarily focused on measurable risk reduction, which was discussed earlier in this chapter. Among the specific financial metrics to measure the quality of a security program, you can consider the following:

- Risk reduction measured in financial terms, such as incidents avoided
- New revenue made possible by improved security practices
- Improvements in the business alignment of security and business processes

A practical way of getting a handle on some of this data is to use scenario planning. To start this process, consider the past incidents that the organization has experienced alongside their frequency and actual impact. Then, imagine that, during these incidents, one or more of the controls had failed. Now, consider the impact the same incident would have had under that scenario.

It is also possible, and useful, to expand this scenario planning into a tabletop exercise that runs through a scenario on paper and aims to determine what the organizational response to events would be. This gives a good handle on missing elements in the incident response plan but can also serve to socialize the potential consequences of a cyber incident.

> **Note**
>
> As an example of this, consider malware that's been stopped by the malware software. What would the consequence be if the malware had been able to execute? What would the next control be under that scenario?

Such scenarios can give us a handle on both the potential impact of incidents, as well as the cost-effectiveness of the various controls that are being used in the business.

We'll look at customer metrics next.

Customer metrics

As a set of customer metrics, we may consider the following:

- Cyber-attacks that are avoided by controls. For instance, filtering at the border stops many email-borne spam and malware attacks that would cost time and effort to resolve if they made it into the environment.

- Vulnerabilities affecting customer environments and the speed with which they are addressed.

- The quality and quantity of cyber advice to users in the environment.

Customers are somewhat hard to define in the context of a cybersecurity program, but in organizations that do not sell software products or IT services, they generally consist of end users in the environments we defend.

Operations metrics

Most organizations measure cybersecurity primarily in terms of operations metrics: vulnerabilities patched, the amount of malware removed by the detection and response software, or the number of bad emails held in the queues at the border.

> **Note**
>
> Carson Zimmerman defined several robust metrics to measure the effectiveness of security operations (`https://www.fireeye.com/content/dam/fireeye-www/summit/cds-2019/presentations/cds19-executive-s03b-practical-soc-metrics.pdf`). Not all these metrics are what you would expect, and it is an illuminating exercise to consider whether you can implement these controls in your environment and how useful that might be.

We can subdivide these operations metrics into **control effectiveness** and **detection effectiveness**.

Measuring control effectiveness

The control framework is the series of controls, alongside the frequency with which they are monitored. As an example, an organization may opt to review failed logons every day and report on the top five accounts that generate the most failed logins. Such an activity is called a control, and the documentation of all controls is known as the control framework.

Control effectiveness measures several aspects of the control framework, such as the following:

- **Coverage**: The ATT&CK framework gives us a clue about how well all our controls cover the known and documented TTPs of attack groups. In addition, coverage can be measured as a percentage of the systems that fall under the control framework.

- **Feed health**: Feed health monitors the current state of the data feed that underlies the generation of alerts. Feed health considers, for instance, whether the feed is still up and running, as well as whether the format of the feed can still be parsed by the software that generates the alerts.

- **Up-to-dateness**: When was the control framework last reviewed?

Control effectiveness is not regularly monitored by many teams but is an important factor in determining the effectiveness of security operations. Logging deficiencies and gaps in the controls that are being monitored by a security team are major contributors to difficulties during forensics.

Measuring detection and response effectiveness

Some measurements for detection and response might be as follows:

- Incident resolution across each phase of the incident response cycle. How long does it take to detect an incident? What detected the incident? How long did it take to analyze? Did the analysis lead to another detection? How long does an incident take to resolve?

- The speed of incident resolution is indexed by the frequency of the incident. Incidents that occur frequently should be resolved fast. The cadence of response should be faster for incidents that occur more frequently.

- Detection effectiveness. With a mature detection engineering practice, it is also possible to develop a metric of how often certain detections produce an alert and whether these were false or true positives.

This discussion of control effectiveness and detection and response effectiveness completes our section on operations metrics. This also reinforces the fact that what matters in security operations is detection and response capabilities.

Metrics for capabilities

The capabilities dimension measures the personnel of the security operation. Generally, capabilities are measured through the maturity model of an organization. For security operations, several freely available maturity models are available.

> **Maturity Models for Security Operations**
>
> There are several maturity models for security operations, among which is the SOC CMM by Rob van Os (https://soc-cmm.com/) and the Open CSIRT SIM3 model (https://opencsirt.org/csirt-maturity/sim3-and-references/).

Some metrics that may be useful, as well as easy to measure and record, are as follows:

- Training
- Experience
- Trust group membership

These are just some examples of metrics that may be useful in measuring the effectiveness and value of agile security operations. There is no doubt that more could be measured, and that context determines, in large, what is useful to measure.

Summary

In this chapter, we looked at several elements that make up the risk management and strategy components of security operations. We discussed how, for some of these, we can bring in an element of agility to connect to the agility needed in security operations.

This chapter also concludes *Part 2* of this book, which focused on the basic aspects of implementing agile security operations.

Much of what we discussed in *Part 2* forms the foundation for *Part 3*. In the next chapter, we will focus on some specific aspects of security operations, such as purple teaming, threat intelligence, and running security operations as a set of services.

Section 3: Advanced Agile Security Operations

Part 3 focuses on the integration of agile security operations with some of the more "traditional" approaches in security: blue and purple teaming, running security as a set of services, and how to implement a threat intelligence program.

This part of the book comprises the following chapters:

- *Chapter 8, Red, Blue, and Purple Teaming*
- *Chapter 9, Running and Operating Security Services*
- *Chapter 10, Implementing Agile Threat Intelligence*

8
Red, Blue, and Purple Teaming

Active defense, which we discussed in *Chapter 6, Active Defense*, applies the principles of blue teaming. Many organizations, as part of the process of deploying new applications, as well as to provide ongoing assurance, perform red teaming to ensure that at least the obvious security vulnerabilities have been addressed before putting a new application or a new infrastructure out into the world. Purple teaming is a mix of the two.

In purple teaming, the defenders, or the blue team, perform monitoring and alerting, while the red team, the attackers, perform controlled attacks. During the process or afterward, the teams compare notes to evaluate how certain attacks appear on the network, whether detections need to be updated, and whether defenses need to be strengthened in certain areas. The business value of purple teaming is that it allows an organization to gradually move to threat-informed defense.

A purple team adds a certain amount of adversity to a blue team. Purple teaming aims to give a direct answer to the question, *Are we vulnerable?*, in ways that can be directly communicated to the business.

This chapter will outline how organizations can get the most out of purple teaming by covering the following topics:

- Red teaming and blue teaming
- Purple teaming concepts

- Purple teaming operations

- Closing into threat informed defense

The MITRE ATT&CK framework is a key tool in the practice of purple teaming. ATT&CK enumerates known attack techniques and can also be used as a tool to simulate attacks. ATT&CK can be used to create attack playbooks and enumerate tactics, techniques, and procedures. If you want to create an advanced attack and test that, ATT&CK will also assist you in developing scenarios.

Red teaming and blue teaming

In this section, we'll develop a view of what purple teaming is by considering the operations of a red team, a blue team, and a purple team.

The context for a blue team, in terms of our closure of the incident loop, which we discussed in *Chapter 3, Engineering for Incident Response*, is given in the following diagram.

The purpose of a blue team is to improve the security posture by preventing breaches, improve the discovery of breaches by providing better detection, and improve how breaches are analyzed and contained. The main purpose of purple teaming is to give the blue team an expanded approach to do just that.

The focus points of this chapter are depicted in the following diagram, which, as you might notice, is an extract of the agile incident response loop we discussed in *Chapter 3, Engineering for Incident Response.*

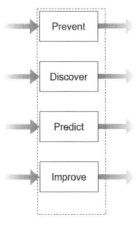

Figure 8.1 – Context of blue and purple teaming

There are several ways in which the blue team can test its execution and solicit meaningful feedback. One way is through a tabletop exercise, which runs through the processes and communication channels for incident response without involving the technical side of an incident. Another way a blue team can test their technical capabilities for detection is by performing a red team exercise. A red team is a team of adversaries executing a friendly attack – that is, an attack that, if successful, does not have the usual undesirable consequences of a cyber-attack.

Why red team?

The purpose of a red teaming exercise is to exercise the defensive posture of an organization, find the weak spots in people, processes, and technology that may negatively impact the performance of the team during incident response, and expose vulnerabilities that may have been missed during penetration testing.

Another benefit of performing a red team exercise is that it is an end-to-end real-life simulation of how the organization may be compromised, using a range of existing vulnerabilities and chaining them into an attack path.

What is a red team?

In the early days, red teaming was largely made up of manual processes, based on a combination of penetration testing, sometimes accompanied by physical intrusion. Red teams focus on behaving like the bad guys, and finding and exploiting vulnerabilities is their day job.

A red team has expertise in compromise techniques and taking an adversarial view on the environment.

A red team performs adversary tactics, techniques, and procedures in a non-adversarial way on a target environment, thereby gaining an understanding of how well that target environment can deal with the specifics of that type of attack.

> **Note**
>
> An interesting website with red team guides is `https://redteam.guide/`.

Activities that a red team may perform include penetration testing, physically entering premises, phone calls or voice solicitation, wardriving, or performing network intrusions through the internet. A red team will display all adversary behaviors without the consequences.

What a red team brings to the business is real-life validation of the defensive approach and proof that the defenses work (or not).

The problem with manual red teaming is that it is an expensive exercise that is moreover focused on only some aspects of the attack paths and vulnerabilities of an organization. The most frequent problems with the red team approach to security are as follows:

- It's difficult to close the loop between red team findings and blue team defenses, leading to a situation in which repeated red team exercises can find the same problems that haven't been fixed.

- The red team, when working in isolation, has few opportunities to strengthen their skills.

- It is hard or even impossible to determine how good security operations function overall from a single red team exercise.

- A single red team exercise does not give a robust view of the security posture of an organization.

In summary, repeated red team exercises are unlikely to make defenses or red team skills better without a concerted effort to close the loop, retest defenses once they've been improved, and retest the skills of the red team against these improved defenses.

More recently, the work of red teaming is performed through attack **simulation**, which mimics the effects of an attack on our environment. We'll discuss this later in this chapter.

What is a blue team?

The blue team is the defender team and uses a combination of controls or passive defense, as well as active defense, as discussed in *Chapter 6, Active Defense*.

The strengths of a blue team are as follows:

- They know the business context of the environment. That is, for a given system, the blue team knows why that system is there and what it is doing.

- They know the architecture of the environment, and hence have a map of the landscape.

- They are experts in detection and response engineering.

Before we delve into the details of purple teaming, we'll look at handling some of the intricacies of the alert stream, as well as how blue teams best handle how to improve detections and alerts. This will allow us to discuss **threat hunting** as a required blue team activity before we get into purple teaming.

Threat hunting

Threat hunting is an activity that's performed by the blue team that seeks to find (and destroy) specific threats on a network. Sometimes, threat hunting is also described as dealing with the unknown unknowns: the adversaries you didn't know you had. Threat hunting is a structured process for flushing these adversaries out of the network if they are there.

Threat hunting builds on this process by creating a practice in the blue team that focuses specifically on the unknown. Since threat hunting deals with the unknown, we need a **hunt lead** to tell us what to hunt for. As we'll discuss next, two sources of hunt leads exist: analytic queries across the security data, which aim to uncover any activity that has escaped detection up to this point, or a more in-depth analysis of the alert stream.

Hunt leads

A good question that blue teams engaging with threat hunting need to ask themselves is: *What do we need to hunt for*? In *Chapter 3, Engineering for Incident Response*, as well as in *Chapter 6, Active Defense*, we briefly discussed the business model of attackers and how work is distributed in the cybercrime ecosystem. The division of labor that is introduced in this way leads to some clues that we may use to develop hunt queries.

As an example, for some steps in the kill chain, attack groups may use similar tools or register the links they want their victims to click on with the same registrar each time. This can be used by the defenders to systematically search for links in incoming emails that match the top-level domain extensions that were used by this same group in the past.

The fact that the cybercrime ecosystem is distributed among many players, with some activities outsourced to specific groups, gives defenders an additional advantage. Outsourcing works best if there are agreed and identical deliverables, and there is a high likelihood, although no certainty, that similarities exist between attacks facilitated by outsourcing groups.

Threat intelligence reports may also give us a reliable source of hypotheses about how to detect the activity of attack groups. These hypotheses are turned into analytic queries.

Analytic queries

Hunting leads do not usually result from normal alerts; they are usually the result of performing specific analytic queries on the available data, which is spurred on by a leading question. This leading question often focuses on the **outliers** in the environment, something that is missed by alerts configured in the SIEM, but which nevertheless may need investigation.

Hunt leads or **analytic queries** scan a large amount of security data, including logs, network data, security events, endpoint security events, and more for the presence of indicators that a security event has occurred. Another way of stating this is that an analytic query translates a hypothesis or leading question into a specific investigation on already existing security data.

Examples of leading questions include how much is PowerShell used in my environment, what is PowerShell typically used for, and what do outliers in PowerShell look like? Another leading question may be whether something interesting can be observed in the least resolved DNS queries from the business (such as leading to sites that are visited rarely or only by one or two individuals), or looking at the least frequently loaded drivers in a Windows environment.

Apart from hypotheses about the internal workings of attack groups, activities on the network that, for several reasons, we might believe to have a negative impact may form another useful source of analytic or hunt queries. An example of that could be excessive amounts of failed logins, lookups on our DNS servers to sites related to malware, or the use of PowerShell in Windows environments.

Alternative hunt leads – alert streams and detections

In *Chapter 3, Engineering for Incident Response*, we discussed the difference between alerting and pulling detections. However, we left this somewhat open regarding when and how these different approaches should be performed.

Alerting was covered from the viewpoint of a security incident management perspective, where predetermined sequences of events set off an alert that is then investigated by the security team. As we discussed, the problem with alerting is alert fatigue, where the firehose of alerts overwhelms the security team, and a tendency to under-investigate events develops because the false positives become too much to deal with.

As a radical approach, we proposed a method where security teams could **pull events** from the stream and investigate them in depth, in addition to maintaining alerting coverage. The advantage of the latter method is that such in-depth investigation will lead to better analysis of root causes of incidents and the hygienic approaches that may be necessary to prevent such incidents from occurring in the future.

The events that a security team will typically pull do not lead to alarms or tickets and are, in most cases, not regularly investigated as part of the ongoing monitoring activity. The preferred events to focus on in this activity are ones that are poorly understood or need a significant amount of work to determine the cause.

So, it seems a detection strategy for a blue team will be a balance between two approaches, which are outlined in the following diagram:

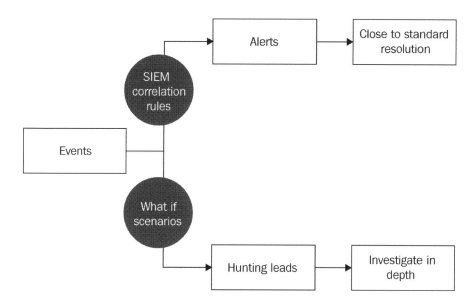

Figure 8.2 – The difference between an alert push and an alert pull

The tradeoff is that, on one hand, the security team needs to ensure that they are regularly checking alerts to ensure that they are acted on, while on the other hand, it is also necessary to investigate alerts outside this group to ensure that no new methods of attack are being developed inside the organization that might go undetected.

The events that are investigated in depth may, in turn, lead to the creation of new correlation rules or detections. Once the context of an event is understood, the team can decide on whether these events need to be part of the things that are checked daily, or whether it is safe to continue ignoring them. Alternatively, this in-depth investigation may uncover configuration issues or poor operational practices that need to be addressed.

This is all part of the feedback loop of an agile process.

A basic quandary

The distinction between alert pushing and pulling does not deal with a basic quandary: how does the blue team decide which types of alerts are worth pulling?

There are broadly two answers to this conundrum: the blue team can implement threat hunting or purple teaming.

In threat hunting, the blue team can ask *what-if* questions and use these as hypotheses or hunting leads in the threat hunting process, which we discussed previously. The threat hunting process focuses on the unknown unknowns: the team does not know whether there is activity by an unknown threat actor that doesn't generate alerts on their network and sets out to systematically discover this and respond to it.

In purple teaming, the team builds out a practice of threat-informed defense to develop a picture of how the network would stand up to a known actor and test their defenses. In contrast to threat hunting, which focuses on the unknown unknowns, purple teaming focuses on the known unknowns: the known activities of a threat actor having an unknown impact on the network.

From this perspective, both threat hunting and purple teaming are structured methods for discovering alerts that may have been previously overlooked but that are useful in the context of the organization.

Managing alert stream quality

There is a balance between ensuring a reasonable daily coverage and in-depth investigation. The treatment strategy for these two approaches is also different. In a stream where alerts are pushed onto an analyst, we'll need to look at automation and orchestration to make sure that each alert can be handled in the minimum time available.

For the daily checks, which consist of an alert stream of pushed alerts, we try to minimize the *work* associated with handling an event. The key principle is that a team needs to manage alert fatigue.

> **Note**
> **Alert fatigue** is one of the major threats to a security operations program and results from teams having to chase many alerts that are of low quality, have a high false-positive rate, and are poorly or not actionable: nothing can be done to fix the incidence of the alert and it will reappear tomorrow and the day after that, and generate a new service ticket each time it reappears.

The key success factors are as follows:

- **Automation**: Try to automate how an event is handled as much as possible to reduce the workload associated with an event.
- **Standardization**: Ensure that each alert is resolved in a standard way.

- **Regularity**: Ensure that these tasks are done on schedule.
- Manage alert fatigue by ensuring that the alert stream is of high quality and actionable.

A system of daily checks will not be enough by itself to keep an organization safe. In addition to such checks, organizations need to investigate some alerts that fall outside of the scope of the daily checks and investigate them in depth. The aim is to try to analyze the root cause of the event to minimize the *number* of events that need to be dealt with.

So, for an alert push, we try to manage the *work* associated with an event, whereas for alerts outside of the alert stream, we try to manage the *number* of alerts. This still leaves a few questions that we'll need to discuss.

The first of these is how to ensure sufficient coverage of important events in the daily checks. The key to answering this question lies in improving and managing the quality of the alert stream.

Most security tooling has a dashboard that summarizes and groups the events the tool deems to be the most important. This will be a good starting point if nothing else is available to the team, but it is also important that the starting point will be gradually evolved into a posture that is meaningful to the type of threats an organization is facing.

A three-pronged approach to alert stream quality improvement is as follows:

1. Reduce alert fatigue by improving detection quality.
2. Use automation and orchestration to reduce the workload associated with those alerts that remain.
3. Unearth new important alerts.

Now, let's look at each of these in turn.

Reduce alert fatigue by improving detection quality

The first step of this evolution consists of gradually weeding out the alert fatigue that may result from working with a relatively standardized set of alerts appearing in the dashboard.

Alerts that frequently lead to false positives or are non-actionable should be improved or removed. Improving alerts is part of detection engineering, which we've already discussed, and can follow a three-pronged approach:

- Investigate whether the alert is missing important data. Getting all the security and contextual data into a detection tool is often a bigger problem than it first seems, and many security teams wage a daily battle for the logs.

- Investigate whether the alert is based on an incorrect assumption or assessment of the business context. The generalized dashboards that come with many tools make standard assumptions on what is important for the average organization. However, you are not average, and there may be factors at play in your organization that are not reflected in the general assumptions that underlie the standardized version of the alert.

- Remove the alert if the data or contextual information cannot be improved.

Apart from improving the quality of the alerts and weeding out the ones that, in the end, turn out to be mere time-wasters (also known as false positives), we can also look at the workload associated with each alert.

Use automation and orchestration to minimize the workload

The second step of the evolution consists of minimizing the work involved in handling the alerts that remain through automation or orchestration.

> **SOAR**
>
> People often use **Security Orchestration, Automation, and Response (SOAR)** in this context. The automation component refers to some static defensive actions that may be undertaken automatically once an event has been detected, such as disabling accounts that are being abused. Obviously, for automation to work, the team needs a high degree of confidence in the process and an extremely low (preferably zero) false-positive rate.

Generally, a lot is written about how important automation and orchestration are in handling alert fatigue, but there may be distortion at play here. Generally, implementing automation and orchestration will involve paying for and deploying a suite of orchestration tools atop the detection tools that already exist, which leads to an additional income stream for vendors and consultants.

Implementing automation and orchestration also requires that the security tools that we deploy in the business can integrate with each other. In general, REST APIs may be used to pass information from one tool to another.

> **Note**
>
> Sometimes, people confuse integration with consolidation, where all the data ends up in a single tool. As a design philosophy, integration is preferable to consolidation because the time and effort involved in getting all the data into a single tool, in many cases, outweigh the benefits of having everything in one place. Once a team is in the process of investigating an alert, looking up the details in an authoritative source system is only a small overhead.

Unearth new, important alerts

The last step consists of unearthing alerts that are not reflected on the dashboard but are important in the context of the organization.

It is for this reason that the event pull approach is important: this approach will give us rapid access to contextualized threats that are important to the organization.

Detection engineering can be used to turn pulled alerts into regular checks, which are checked and reported as part of the ongoing maintenance of the security baseline. In this way, pulled alerts may become **hunting leads**.

Implementing a threat hunting practice

Now is a good time to discuss how to implement a threat hunting practice and connect it to the framework we've built in this book.

Approach

Since threat hunting deals primarily with unknown unknowns, in terms of the Cynefin model we discussed in *Chapter 4, Key Concepts in Cyber Defense*, threat hunting belongs in the **complex** domain, where the best approach is to **probe**, **sense**, and then **respond**. Let's discuss the approaches that are relevant to the specific threat hunting practices:

- **Probe**: The threat hunting process focuses on investigating a small number of outlier events, or specific what-if scenarios defined as analytic queries, called hunt leads, in depth, which are deliberately pulled from the events available or systematically searched for.

- **Sense**: Then, it investigates these events in depth and correlates them with what is known about the threats. In some cases, these events can be linked to a hitherto unknown threat, while in other cases, the events will correspond to normal events in the context of our business. The remainder of cases may be attributable to operational hygiene: stuff that should have been cleaned up long ago but is still hanging around.

- **Respond**: Based on the outcome of the hunt, the response can vary from having a new threat group to track, to doing nothing, to cleaning up our operational act.

To support this approach, we need to implement several practices that, taken together, define the process of threat hunting.

Required practices

The following practices are required to support a threat hunting capability:

- **Hunt leads**: You can also think about a hunt lead as a hypothesis. Generate hunt leads based on the development of analytic queries capable of detecting malicious activity on the security data or start pulling unloved detections from the alert stream for further investigation in detail.

- **Investigation**: The next step is to investigate the evidence. Consider data that is required to do a proper investigation and where it is stored, as well as how easily it can be accessed by the security team. During this step, also consider (as a side note) whether data that is not already part of the data that's been collected for regular security activities should be collected in the future. Then, iteratively mine the data for evidence that either supports or disproves the hypothesis.

- **Response**: Respond to the results of the investigation, whether this is dealing with attacks that were undiscovered up to now, operational gaps that need to be addressed, or architecture and passive defenses that need strengthening.

- **Intelligence**: If there are new threat groups to track, define new patterns and TTPs and enrich analytics, and perform detection engineering to update the standard set of alerts on the SIEM.

Threat hunting may look like incident response but is different in significant respects. In a threat hunt, there is no detectable impact of a security incident to track during the hunting process, whereas an incident response process is usually triggered because of either an alert or some noticeable impact on our infrastructure. The result is different too. An incident response process resolves an incident and recovers from its impact, while threat hunts test a hypothesis. In other words, some hunts do not deliver the discovery of new threat activity on our network.

Realizing value

In terms of maintaining and improving our security posture, threat hunting makes two important contributions: it allows us to detect the activity of a previously unknown threat group, and it allows us to improve our operational hygiene, which contributes significantly to improving the security baseline.

We can take threat hunting a step further and simulate attacks instead of hunting for the presence of intruders on our networks. In the next section, we will discuss mixing red and blue teams to form purple teaming, one of the activities that can help improve the quality of the alert stream and lead to an improved security posture.

Purple teaming concepts

When we mix the colors red and blue, we get purple. Due to this, mixing the activities of a red and blue team is referred to as **purple teaming**. Like threat hunting, purple teaming is also an activity that forms part of active defense. A purple team is not a team. Purple teaming is an *activity*, undertaken jointly by the red and blue teams, that combines the strengths of both the red team and the blue team and aims to speed up the improvement of the security posture.

Purple team activities

In terms of the Cynefin framework, which we discussed in *Chapter 4, Key Concepts in Cyber Defense*, this places it in the **complex** domain, like threat hunting. Again, the best approach is to **probe**, **sense**, and then **respond**. Purple teaming uses a structured approach to probing our networks, applications, and infrastructure in an organized red side of the team, and the purple teaming process is designed to optimize the sensitivity and response qualities of our security team, as follows:

- **Probe**: The red side of the purple team generates attacks on our applications or infrastructure in a non-adversarial, controlled manner that is designed to have no impact on the infrastructure.
- **Sense**: The blue side of the team then investigates whether these probing attacks generate alerts or events and reports back to the red team with their detections, also in a controlled manner.
- **Respond**: In this phase, the red and blue sides of the team do a joint debrief to determine how to improve the detection and response capabilities, or even write new detections for events that did go unnoticed.

A purple team is a team in which the activities of defense and attack interact to create an approach to threat-driven defense. From that perspective, in the remainder of this chapter, we will talk about the blue side and the red side of the purple teaming activity.

Characteristics of blue and red teams

A purple teaming activity consists of a red side and a blue side, each focused on executing attack scenarios and improving defenses, respectively. As such, a purple team is not a team – it is an activity that is undertaken by defenders, red teamers, operations, and management. Purple teaming is more an activity than a separate team in the organization. A purple team will not be found on the organizational chart.

The characteristics of the blue and red sides that can be combined into the purple team activities are as follows:

- Highly agile in both red and blue operations. Purple teaming relies on continuous feedback, regular communication, and iterative improvements. It can be made more efficient if we can also fail fast. In this context, this means updating detections iteratively during the engagement, perhaps repeating some aspects of the engagement as the situation evolves.

- The ability to work from a plan. While this may seem to contradict the agile side of purple teaming, it is still a planned activity.

- Effective communication skills.

- Focused on continuous improvement.

A purple teaming exercise aims to enhance the security posture, and as such, purple teaming relies heavily on a mature blue team, which has the basics of detection, response, and detection engineering already developed. The most important feature of a blue team that will allow the organization to benefit from a purple teaming exercise is that the team is capable of rapidly improving its detection and reporting capabilities, and updating the detections as needed.

In opposition to a reasonably mature blue team operation, the red side of the purple teaming operation may only require the ability to perform some type of adversary operation. From this perspective, rather than performing a manual and highly involved red team exercise, all that may be required here is a basic capability, although the expectation is that during the purple teaming exercise, the red side will get better at what it does.

Agile approaches to purple teaming

Almost by definition, the purple teaming activity is set up to execute various agile methodologies, including rapid feedback for both the red side and the blue side of the team, and continuous learning and continuous improvement of the security posture.

Purple teaming operations

Several activities make up the purple team's tasks. As is clear from our discussion in the previous section, a purple team performs the combined activities of red and blue teams. The aim is to improve defenses by discovering, communicating, and mitigating findings on attack paths and vulnerabilities. Purple teaming is an activity that is focused on continuously improving the security posture.

The purple teaming activity consists of a structured process with regular feedback:

1. The red side of the team runs a simulated attack.

2. The attack is either prevented, detected, or remains undetected and is executed. In the first two cases, the red side of the team receives a report from the blue side at the scheduled interactions.

3. Non-detected attacks or simulations lead to a report from the red side of the team to the blue side, which contains details of the attack that slipped through.

4. At the end of the exercise, the red and blue sides of the team do a joint debrief or **hotwash** that focuses on improvements that can be made to the cybersecurity posture.

The purple teaming process is shown in the following diagram:

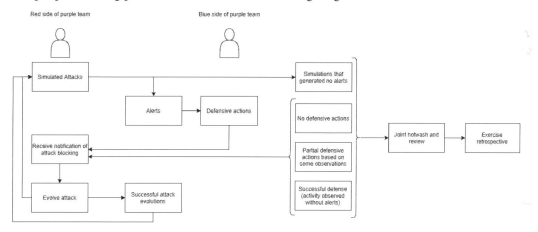

Figure 8.3 – The purple teaming workflow

In the execution of this cycle, we need to consider which attack simulations to run, how to run them, and how to improve detections for them, should the blue team not pick up the attempts made by the red side of the team. Hence, planning and preparation is a key activity in purple teaming: specifically, the purple teaming exercise should have a mission plan that defines what type of attacks or attacker groups will be simulated, the time frame for the exercise, including planned interactions between the red and blue sides, any conflict resolution procedures, and a process for running the hotwash.

Planning – sources of attack data

When it comes to selecting attack data, an organization can use several sources.

Incident response closure

For any organization, past incident data is a reliable guide to at least part of the future incident response process. Many cyber-criminal organizations focus on specific sectors of the economy, or a specific vertical, and will attack that vertical regularly. If the organization has developed a library of past incidents and how they were dealt with, it can use this as a guide to developing plans for attack simulations.

Past incidents can be used to further develop attack scenarios if a control failed or is not available or by assuming that an attacker will continuously improve and, at some point, be able to circumvent one or more of our controls that have successfully stopped them in the past.

Threat intelligence and news reports

An organization may look at news reports and focus on groups that have attacked their competitors (provided the group has been identified in the report). Further research with publicly available resources may then reveal some of the methods that have been used by the attackers, which can then be used to guide the purple team exercise.

Threat groups from ATT&CK

The ATT&CK framework contains a list of attack groups that have been tracked by MITRE, which contains some details about the sectors that are commonly targeted by such groups, along with their preferred Tactics, Techniques, and Procedures.

Planning – cadence and process

Before you implement the purple teaming process, several things need to be decided first.

Attacker to simulate

The ATT&CK framework will help us select an attack simulation scenario. As an example, we may choose to simulate (part of) the activities of a particular threat group during an exercise. The ATT&CK framework can be used to generate a playbook for that purple teaming exercise, with a list of **Tools, Tactics and Procedures (TTPs)** that are typically used by that threat group, as well as the sequencing of such an attack.

Pacing

As we plan for sprints in the agile methodology, we need to plan the interactions between the blue and red sides when executing the purple teaming process.

At the interaction points, the red side of the team informs the blue side of which attack simulations were run successfully (from the attacker's perspective) and which one the red side believes has failed and how. The blue side then has an opportunity to work on its detection engineering for the attack simulations that were successful and improve on its detection and response.

Conflicts

During the execution, there may be conflicts between the red and blue sides or conflicts between the needs of the purple team and the wider operational needs of the business. It is important to establish prior principles to resolve such conflicts. These may include the following:

- The conditions under which the simulation can be stopped (for instance, where it interferes with operations or is unsafe to continue).

- A strong emphasis on the fact that the purple teaming exercise is a joint exercise, not a contest.

- Decide on a person with executive authority who can arbitrage conflicts and whose decision is final. This person is sometimes called a **white team**.

With the plan documented, we can execute the plan.

Executing the red side of purple teaming

Once we have an attack that we want to simulate, it is time to execute the purple teaming exercise. We must start by planning out a scenario.

Red team attacks

It is possible to have an actual red team perform the attack during a purple teaming exercise. The attacks can be sophisticated. What is important, however, is that the red side of the team receives feedback on whether the attack succeeded or not. The red side of the team can then use that information to determine the next steps.

Phishing simulations

Many organizations run simulated phishing on their users, which you may see as the beginnings of a purple team approach. In simulated phishing, an outside organization, or the security team themselves, sends email messages to the user base with benign phishing links. Users that click on the links can be gently steered toward some more phishing training. In addition, the organization gathers data on the percentage of its users that are phish-prone to target its end user policies and education.

Attack simulations

We can go one step further and simulate an actual attack with multiple stages by following a defined playbook that can be derived, for instance, from the documented behavior of one of the known adversary groups with MITRE ATT&CK.

> **Note**
>
> The open source project known as MITRE Caldera lets us execute simulated attacks by following a defined playbook. This can be found at `https://caldera.mitre.org/`.

Once the basic details of the attack scenario have been documented, we need to develop the scenario that the blue and red teams are going to work with during purple teaming in detail, including how the information will be shared between the red side and the blue side of the team.

Feedback – moving to an agile approach

The simulated attack either succeeds or doesn't. If it does succeed, the red side of the team informs the blue side of the event, allowing the blue side of the team to improve their defenses through detection engineering. If the attack fails for some reason, the red team may decide to launch a variation of the attack to see if that is successful.

An important aspect of the feedback loop is that we manage the schedule of the exercise to ensure that feedback loops can occur at each stage of the attack simulation cycle. The stages of the attack simulation cycle are determined by the TTPs of the attacker we want to simulate.

As an example, if we want to simulate the activities of threat group FIN8, we can select that threat group from the **Groups** tab of the attack website (`https://attack.mitre.org`), which will give us a list of the TTPs that are typically used by this group. We can then use this list to set up a model for the attack for the red side of the team to emulate.

In terms of timing, we can plan the exercise in such a way that, for instance, the intrusion stage of the attack takes 3 days, during which the red side of the team will try the methods of FIN8 on the network, giving the blue side of the team a chance to detect, respond, and improve their detections progressively.

In the next stage, we may move on to the *execution*, *persistence*, and *privilege escalation* phases of the attack.

In this way, a purple teaming exercise can systematically exercise the activities of an attack group on their network. A drawback of this method is that a real attack would not be timed that tidily. This is a consequence of the fact that the attack is a simulation, and since it is a part of the simulation we have built a specific timing and feedback opportunity that does not exist in real-life attacks.

It should not take much to recognize the key elements of an agile approach in this process:

- The teams manage the schedule of the exercise, ensuring that there is a certain element of pacing in the overall exercise and that we don't get stuck.
- Communication and feedback are key to the whole thing.
- The purple teaming get-togethers are no-blame exercises that focus on continuously improving detection and response.

Purple teaming forms part of an approach to cyber defense that is commonly called threat-informed defense.

Closing into threat-informed defense

The purpose of a purple team exercise is to ensure that we close the various feedback loops of the simulation into a threat-informed defense scenario, where the readiness of an organization to respond to real-life attacks is measured and systematically improved.

Business value from purple teaming

A robust purple team approach to security has many advantages; among them are a better approach to threat informed defense, robust security baselining, and overall improvements in the security posture. In terms of the strategy models we discussed in *Chapter 7, How Secure Are You? - Measuring Security Posture*, purple teaming is a key capability that delivers better security from the customer and risk perspectives.

Security baselining

One of the key strategic questions is, as discussed earlier in this book, how secure the organization is. As we have seen in *Chapter 7, How Secure Are You? – Measuring Security Posture*, this question boils down to the risk the organization runs with both its current operations and its new initiatives.

A purple teaming exercise delivers a clear view of the amount of risk buydown resulting from new initiatives, as well as articulating whether the organization has a workable baseline. That is, is the current risk in line with what is acceptable, given the development of new types of attacks? Purple teaming allows organizations to test these scenarios in real life. During purple teaming, the organization can articulate this risk by considering the resilience of the organizational defenses against specific attacks and then map out where the current defenses fail and need improvement.

In other words, as attacks develop and evolve, purple teaming gives an organization a strong insight into where the security baseline needs improvement.

Security posture improvement

We can see purple teaming as a coordinated effort to improve the quality of the alert stream of the security team so that critical events can be noted, managed, and acted on. In this way, purple teaming, as an activity, contributes to threat-informed defense.

Threat-informed defense

Threat-informed defense is an approach in which the defenses that an organization deploys are tailored to the threats it faces so that the security spend is optimized, and the risk of known threats is reduced.

Threat-informed defense focuses on having a deep understanding of the effects that threat groups have on the infrastructure of our business. It should be executed alongside, not in place of, a program to maintain a core security baseline, and should be informed by a combination of a deep understanding of the business and systems landscapes with the activities that various threat groups perform and the impact they can have on the business.

The success factors for threat-informed defense are as follows:

- Threat-informed defense works alongside an already existing program and does not take the place of basic maintenance of the security posture. A program that is unable to measure and maintain a baseline will not be ready to engage with threat-informed defense.

- Threat-informed defense is based on a deep understanding of the behavior and objectives of specific attack groups, as well as the context of the business.

- Threat-informed defense is actively used to improve incident response playbooks and practices, as well as in detection engineering.

An important aspect of executing threat-informed defense is threat intelligence, which is what we'll discuss in *Chapter 10*, Implementing *Agile Threat Intelligence*.

Summary

In this chapter, we discussed the concepts behind red teaming, blue teaming, and purple teaming and how they can be combined into a threat-informed defense strategy. This is a practice that should only be engaged in once a robust program to measure and maintain the security baseline has been implemented.

To do purple teaming well, the security team will need a robust monitoring and detection engineering program, as well as active defense capabilities. They will also need a small number of additional people so that they can optimize the workload so that it aligns with this strategy.

The improvements that can be made with this strategy will lead to significant improvements in the security posture of the business. In the next chapter, we will discuss security services.

9
Running and Operating Security Services

So far, what we have discussed revolves around the internal aspects of security operations and the internal organization of security teams. In this chapter, the focus will be on the external interactions – what we called the customer perspective in *Chapter 7, How Secure Are You? – Measuring Security Posture*.

To consider this topic, we will think of security operations as a set of services delivered to the business. As we outlined earlier, the customer's perspective of security operations revolves around the amount of trust an organization has in its security operations, as well as how well security operates as a team player in new business initiatives. In this chapter, we will flesh this out by defining a set of security services that organizations can implement alongside the other services provided by their digital (or IT) teams.

Many organizations struggle with cybersecurity because they do not understand what essential cybersecurity services are.

Security, done well, revolves around six different security services. In this chapter, I will describe these services and why they are necessary, as well as how you can implement them in security operations. Running a credible security program requires that all these six services are covered.

The six services that we'll discuss are not all part of security operations but cover the entire security program, including the strategy, policies, deployment practices, and architecture, besides the services that are implemented as part of security operations, which focus on monitoring, alerting, and incident response.

Defining services in the context of an agile or DevOps environment is very important: it allows service strategies to be developed for these services and also allows you to monitor and evaluate these services, just like any other IT service.

In this chapter, we'll cover the following topics:

- The essential security services
- Service maturity
- Agile approaches to the six security services

The essential security services

In this section, we will discuss security operations and modeled services. Considering the role of security as a set of services allows us to think about how security can be embedded into the wider environment, as well as help improve the visibility, effectiveness, and accountability of security initiatives. This approach also helps align the language of security with other areas of the digital environment.

> **Note**
>
> This chapter is somewhat loosely based on a series of blog posts that I wrote for APNIC that have been published on their site at `https://blog.apnic.net/2016/11/18/itil-no-security-speak/`, `https://blog.apnic.net/2017/02/08/extend-itil-six-essential-cybersecurity-services/`, and `https://blog.apnic.net/2017/07/04/implementing-security-set-services/`.

To discuss security operations as a set of services, we must consider what a service is, and then define six essential security services.

What is a service?

The **Information Technology Infrastructure Library** (**ITIL**) has defined a robust set of service templates that can be used to specify the service and service levels and has provided a definition of a service. In this section, we will use this model to articulate security operations as a set of services.

The ITIL definition of a service is as follows:

"*A means of delivering value to customers by facilitating outcomes customers want to achieve, but without the ownership of specific costs and risks.*"

In *Chapter 7, How Secure Are You? – Measuring Security Posture*, we discussed the customer's perspective on security operations and defined this as the level of trust in an environment. We also looked at what role security plays in developing new business initiatives, such as forming the guardrails that allow businesses to go faster.

Six services make up security operations:

- **Strategy service**: What security teams do when they consider how secure they are and how to improve the security posture

- **Policy service**: A service for creating and updating policies

- **Architecture service**: A service for creating security designs and consulting on the security aspects of new and existing applications

- **Deployment service**: A service provided by security to support the deployment of applications and infrastructure, such as setting up monitoring tools, collection strategies, and penetration testing

- **Monitoring service**: The work that's done by the security team to monitor an application every day

- **Incident response service**: How security incidents are initiated and then moved to the incident management process

This is a list that has worked for me in the past, and one that we will continue to use in this chapter. However, it is possible, depending on your circumstances, that more services, such as identity management, certificate management, or code reviews, may be necessary. In terms of the previously mentioned list, code review could also be defined as part of the deployment service.

We will now discuss these in turn. Some of these areas, such as monitoring, incident response, and architecture, will also be discussed in other places in this book, so it may seem like a double-up. What makes the discussion in this chapter different is that we will consider those areas in a service framework; that is, as services that are provided to the rest of the organization by the security team. It is the *services* aspect that is the key focus of this chapter.

Together, the six security services provide a view of what a security program should cover. The first two services – strategy and policies – are, in most organizations, part of the office of the chief information security officer, whereas architecture and deployment are related to how an organization changes its applications and infrastructure. The last two, monitoring and incident response, are part of security operations.

Optionally, some organizations view identity and access management as something that should be operated by their security teams, in which case this needs to be added as a seventh service. All in all, these six services are aligned to the life cycle of applications and infrastructure, encompassing planning, deployment, and operation.

Service worksheets

It is sometimes a good idea to create a **service worksheet** for each service to document the key aspects of what the service entails. The service worksheets, in turn, are collected in a **service catalog**. A service worksheet looks like the following:

Service	Alerting and monitoring service
Definition	The alerting and monitoring service ensures that security events of interest to the organization are continuously monitored and that critical events are turned into alerts which need to be notified and actioned. Criticality of events is determined by correlation rules.
Process	System and application logs are collected with a logging strategy, collected centrally in a searchable data lake. A security incident and event management system applies correlation rules and provides reports, alerts, and some level of orchestration of events. Alerts are triaged and appropriate response is determined.

Service levels	*Business hours*
	    Alerts received immediately
	    Alerts triaged within 15 minutes
	    Monitoring reports generated daily
	Non-business hours
	    Alerts received within 15 minutes
	    Alerts triaged within 30 minutes

Available capacity	1 FTE on site, working with a Managed service security provider
Third party suppliers	MSSP service
Service levels	*Deployment service* to ensure sufficient log management is set up *Incident response* to ensure that alerts are handled
Service practices	Logging strategy Daily reports on events SIEM correlation rule generation and maintenance SIEM orchestration Intergration with service ticketing system Alert ingestion Alert evaluation Alert triage

Figure 9.1 – Service worksheet example

The following is an explanation of some of these items:

- **Service name**: The service should have a name. In the case of security, it should be one of the six security services, although it may also be necessary to include some other services in the security portfolio, such as identity management or certificate management.

- **Definition of the service**: In the definition, we specify what the service is for, what it does, and why it is there. We'll discuss some examples of definitions in the following sections.

- **Process**: The process specifies how the service is executed – specifically, how is the service started, what stages form part of its execution, and how does it end? What are the outputs of the service?

- **Service levels**: Service levels are specifications of how quickly a service runs through the process. As an example, in an identity management service, new identities may be created for new employees. The service level specifies how quickly new accounts will be available to the new employee.

- **Capacity**: The capacity defines the throughput of the service. For instance, can the identity management service create 1,000 new user accounts per day and manage them? Can the incident response service handle two or three concurrent incidents? If so, at what severity?

- **Integration**: Integration defines how the service integrates with other services. For instance, the incident response service will integrate with the monitoring service to detect incidents.

- **Practices**: This is a list of practices that make up the service, as well as the metrics that define how effective the practices are. These practices define what a team *does* to execute a service and allow for the definition of maturity.

With the terms defined, let's see how this works out in practice for the six security services. We will focus on defining some of the practices that make up the security service and the role they play. This sets the stage for your implementation of the security services.

Strategy service

The strategy service sets security strategy along the lines we discussed in *Chapter 7, How Secure Are You? – Measuring Security Posture*. The strategy service aims to define and update security posture alongside the measurement framework, which measures the effectiveness of the security program and the cyber risk of the organization.

As we discussed in *Chapter 7, How Secure Are You? – Measuring Security Posture*, the strategy looks at the articulation of the security strategy. In line with the thinking developed in this book, the security strategy focuses on reducing risk, primarily through increased resilience in dealing with incidents. Incidents where the attackers do not reach their objectives have a diminished impact on the organization and have lessened consequences compared to attacks where the attackers do reach their goals.

Defining the development of strategy as a service also entails that the strategy will be periodically reset and calibrated to past incidents, as well as the current threat landscape.

The strategy service interacts with several other services, especially incident response, to understand the type and impact of past incidents, as well as to gain insight into the impact on events that have occurred in the past.

> **Note**
> Don't underestimate how a proper understanding of past incidents – placing them in the threat landscape overall, assessing their effectiveness from the attacker's point of view, and looking at the organizational impact – can play into the security strategy of an organization, even at the executive level. The experience of an event that has happened usually far outweighs reports of potential impact and abstract risk that *might* happen.

The strategy service considers two specific practices focused on the management of risk.

Strategy practices

Practices that make up the strategy service can be derived from the strategy maps we discussed in *Chapter 7, How Secure Are You? – Measuring Security Posture*, specifically when we discussed **rewarded risk**. This is where security contributes to the business.

The practices that make up the security strategy fall into two broad categories:

- **Risk buydown**: Managing the risk of existing activities and putting controls and practices into place to ensure these risks are manageable.

- **Rewarded risks**: These are the risks that the organization incurs as part of new initiatives and new business development.

The strategy service closely interacts with the incident response service, which it relies on for some of its information on current cyber attacks and how the organization understands them. It also interacts with gathering and processing threat intelligence, which will be discussed in *Chapter 10, Implementing Agile Threat Intelligence*.

Policies

Policies need regular reviewing and updating. The policies service is responsible for creating and reviewing policies.

The definition of the policy service focuses on creating and maintaining a **policy framework** that is aligned to risk, workable from the perspective of IT operations, and has comprehensive coverage.

Policy practices

The practices that make up a policy service are as follows:

- **Policy creation and review**: Creating new policies and regularly reviewing existing policies to ensure they remain relevant.

- **Policy retirement**: Sometimes, policies can be retired as they cover aspects of technology that are no longer relevant to the business.

- **Policy communication**: Policies need to be communicated to their audience.

- **Policy coverage**: This is to ensure that the policy framework adequately covers all the aspects that are relevant to the business.

- **Internal and external audits**: These ensure that policies are operating and adhered to. They document and manage a program of work to remediate policy breaches.

The triggers for these practices can come both from the business (we need a policy for that) or from regular reviews. All policies should be created with review dates, which trigger the update and review process.

Architecture

The security architecture is considering the process of developing specific security components for new solutions, as well as the architecture of the security infrastructure, which is necessary for ongoing monitoring and incident response. We discussed the concept of defensible architecture in *Chapter 5, Defensible Architecture*, but did not consider architecture as a service.

Architecture practices

As a service, architecture has three components, which we label as **practices** in the context of the service:

- The first is the development and maintenance of the security architecture. The security architecture helps you design the elements that enforce the policy (such as authentication and authorization systems), as well as monitor policy enforcement (logging and log analysis, for instance).

- The second is designing the security aspects of the infrastructure and applications. This generally starts with considerations about the risks and the data security needs of the application and infrastructure.

- The third is a consulting service, where the security architect provides advice on good security practices in new and existing initiatives.

One role of the security architect is to ensure that the security baseline of an organization is understood, maintained, and defended.

Deployment

The deployment service focuses on the services provided by a security team to support the deployment of new infrastructure and applications, as well as to help ensure that they are deployed securely and with the right visibility of security events.

Deployment practices

Depending on the process followed by the wider environment, deployment practices can be automated and integrated with a deployment pipeline. Depending on the deployment process that is followed in an organization, several activities are possible. Some examples are as follows:

- **Code review**: Review the code for security vulnerabilities, either with an automated scanner or manually.

- **Scanning**: The simplest practice is to scan the application or infrastructure to be deployed with a standard vulnerability scanner.

- **Security testing**: This testing practice scans the application but also involves manual or automated penetration testing.

Where and how these practices are integrated into the deployment pipeline also depends on how the organization develops and deploys software.

As a rule, performing security tests at the end of a development process is inefficient. A more efficient method is to perform testing alongside the unit and regression tests as part of the QA process.

Monitoring and alerting

The monitoring and alerting service, alongside the incident response service, is at the core of security operations.

Monitoring and alerting activities indicate the work that's typically performed by a **security operations center** (**SOC**). Monitoring and alerting takes logging data from applications and security devices and monitors this data for outliers and outright events. It also manages the quality of the alert stream, something we discussed in *Chapter 8, Red, Blue, and Purple Teaming*.

Monitoring and alerting practices

Examples of some of the practices that make up the monitoring and alerting service are as follows:

- **Alert monitoring**: Checking dashboards.

- **Alert investigation**: Investigating alerts early to see whether they constitute incidents or whether they are false positives.

- **Feed health monitoring**: Checking that the security data feeds are operating as expected.

- **Detection engineering**: Detection engineering, as discussed in *Chapter 3, Engineering for Incident Response*, is the process of developing and improving detections.

- **Security analytics**: This focuses on developing tools to analyze security datasets that might be useful for anomaly detection, detection engineering, and threat hunting.

- **Threat hunting** and **threat intelligence**: These were discussed in *Chapter 8, Red, Blue, and Purple Teaming*, and *Chapter 10, Implementing Agile Threat Intelligence*. The focus of these activities is on threat-informed defense, either by hunting for threats or systemically collecting and operationalizing knowledge about threat groups.

There is a lot more to monitoring and alerting than the examples mentioned in the preceding list. We discussed these in more detail in *Chapter 3, Engineering for Incident Response*, as well as in *Chapter 6, Active Defense*.

Incident response

Even though incident response acts as part of the ITIL incident management component, it is also, in part, a service. The service aspects include response time and response availability, as well as any components of incident response that are used by third parties or other digital teams.

Incident response, as a service, focuses on delivering the necessary knowledge and resources to the business teams affected by the incident. The incident itself is managed through the incident management capabilities that ITIL-aligned organizations have.

Incident response practices

The practices that make up the incident response service are captured in the incident response cycle and were discussed in detail in *Chapter 3, Engineering for Incident Response*, as well as *Chapter 6, Active Defense*.

Other services

The six services we've discussed so far may not be complete. Sometimes, security teams perform other tasks, such as identity and access management, certificate management, or patch and vulnerability management.

Whether you consider these services as part of the security operations or whether they are considered part of normal digital housekeeping is somewhat open for discussion and the predilection of the organization. What is not in doubt, however, is that they can be defined by following the standard service template. Where extra services need to be added, teams can also define services for these activities inside a service framework.

One advantage of clarifying the work of the security team in terms of services is that it becomes easier to discuss the maturity of the services and compare them to the maturity level required by the business. This is something we will discuss next.

Service maturity

As we discussed previously, practices are the components of services. Practices also allow you to define maturity. Maturity can be measured by the practices that make up the services, not the services themselves.

Maturity management

In this section, the focus is on service maturity. The advantages of a defined maturity level for services are twofold: first, it lets the organization decide which maturity level they desire to operate at, and secondly, it provides a roadmap for improvement. Audits and incident response exercises may also identify gaps that need to be remediated.

The key to determining the maturity level of a security service is the **practices** that make up the service. In many cases, practices map back to controls, so it is also possible to say that control maturity is a function of the maturity of a security service, as measured in the number of practices that it implements (provided these implementations meet certain quality standards).

Practices – components of a service

Practices are where the rubber hits the road when a service is delivered. As outlined in the service worksheet shown in *Figure 9.1*, **practices** are the work that's performed to deliver a service. It is also where maturity and effectiveness are measured. Service maturity, for instance, can be classified according to whether delivering the service involves basic or advanced practices, where the distinction between basic and advanced is potentially open to discussion.

We can consider an example to flesh this out. The monitoring and alerting service provides log monitoring, which is a basic practice. Log monitoring is about making sure that you have enough information to troubleshoot any (not just security) issues that occur. Many organizations collect their logs in a **security incident and event monitoring (SIEM)** solution, which, in addition to basic monitoring, can also generate security alerts based on specific combinations of events. This solution can then be built out further to implement **security orchestration, automation, and response (SOAR)** to get to an optimized level of monitoring and alerting. So, we see a progression of basic to advanced practices that help us define the maturity level of a service.

The **interaction** between services also takes place at the level of practices. To build on this example, log monitoring may also start to include hunting for specific indicators of compromise. In an advanced set of practices, this will then be built out further to include things such as threat hunting, threat intelligence feeds, and others, feeding more and more into the incident response service.

The advantage of thinking about maturity in this way is that it allows an organization to sequence their security program and determine what sort of solutions they should be looking to purchase or implement. Generally, the basic practices need to be in place before the more advanced practices are considered. Where log management practices are not up to much, it is a waste of time to be talking to threat intelligence providers.

Measuring effectiveness

One of the advantages of thinking about security operations as a set of services is that it allows you to measure effectiveness. There are generally two common ways to characterize the effectiveness of a service: maturity models and measuring the effectiveness of the service. Effectiveness considers the impact that the service's execution has on the overall security posture.

Maturity models

We can use this to characterize the overall service in terms of a maturity model. The maturity model stipulates a level of maturity that usually ranges from **initial** to **repeatable**, **defined**, **managed**, and **optimized**.

Maturity models usually define a series of levels, running from 0 through to 5, that characterize the maturity of a specific service.

The following table provides a high-level overview of the levels that are commonly found in a maturity model, along with a brief description of the expected maturity of the practices that make up the service:

0	Initial	Usually chaotic, with no documented practices and no training in existing practices
1	Repeatable	Practices are implicit, dependent on individuals in the team, and often not documented
2	Defined	Practices are explicit and documented, and can be executed
3	Managed	Practices are monitored with KPIs
4	Optimized	Continuous improvement to processes and streamlining of efforts

Figure 9.2 – General simplified overview of maturity levels

This table is very high level, and the details of what maturity looks like will need to be worked out service by service and related to the context in which the service is expected to operate.

A common factor is that for security services, the maturity levels are largely defined by the **practices** that constitute the service, as well as how well they are executed. More advanced practices, when executed well, lead to a higher maturity level.

Defining Capability

Another way of looking at the quality of security services is to assess their capability. Capability is partially measured by looking at effectiveness, on the assumption that better capability delivers more effective service. Another way of assessing capability is the interconnections that exist between practices.

Practices across different services work as a matrix, with practices working together to create a full set of security operations. This is a complicated way of saying that one practice depends on another. Specifically, the dependency takes the form of one service producing the necessary data to operate the services that depend on it. While at the surface level it may appear as if the services operated independently, in practice, you need to consider the maturity across the set of services to get a good view of the quality of the program.

As an example, if the monitoring and alerting service is at its initial stage, it is impossible to expect the incident response service to run at the higher levels in the maturity stack, such as managed or optimized, because the data quality that feeds it is most likely going to be poor.

The incident response service is affected by the deficiencies in the monitoring and alerting service at key moments and is starved of visibility and data most of the time.

Maturity does not stand alone

One aspect of security operations should now be clear to you: they are tightly coupled. It is near impossible, for instance, to develop and maintain a mature incident response service based on an immature monitoring and alerting service. Maturity in some services assumes a minimum level of maturity in other services to be fully functional.

Therefore, improvements to the security services should be planned and executed in tandem.

Drawbacks of Maturity

Maturity is a compelling measure in a business context, but not always the best one to have. In this section, we will discuss some of the drawbacks of focusing overly exclusively on the maturity of practices.

There are several reasons why a strong focus on maturity, especially if it's based on standardized models, may carry a cost in terms of effectiveness. These reasons all boil down to the need to have agility in the face of rapidly moving and pivoting attackers. Here are the reasons:

- Maturity models are based on a fixed end goal. This is generally a poor match for security, which is best based on an ongoing process of improvement of practices based on a robust understanding of current attacks and their motivations.

- Hackers are smart and move quickly. Maturity is a poor match for the sort of adversarial landscape that cybersecurity operations face daily.

- Maturity models propose a single road or roadmap to improve maturity. This does not match the variety of business needs and associated security postures that security needs to implement. Moreover, security teams need to be agile to quickly adapt to and engage with attackers.

- A known security end state is incapable of adapting to and incorporating relevant new technologies. A lot of the best security work is done first in open source projects, which deliver real benefits. However, it is hard to adopt such software when the focus is on static roadmaps.

With the limitations discussed in this section, we have seen that maturity is not a static process with an end goal but something that needs continuous alignment with the remainder of the organization. This is what we will discuss in the next section.

Agile approaches to the six security services

The advantage of defining security operations as a set of services is that it can be made to map to the already existing organizational and process structure.

Many organizations have adopted an ITIL framework to deliver digital services to their customers and constituents, but the language of services is stronger: services can be wrapped around agile and DevOps processes too. The articulation of an activity as a service will assist in measuring the agility of that activity.

Now that we've defined the six security services, we can map them to the agile security operations we defined earlier and outline how they fit with agile and DevOps practices.

Agile

Adherence to the agile philosophy will change the culture of a service, not the service itself. The focus will be less on the endless documentation of processes and practices and more on executing the practices themselves.

The services form flexible building blocks that can be integrated with the agile methodology, although doing so needs to be done thoughtfully. There is nothing in the agile, scrum, or Kanban methodologies that enforce security or the integration of security services.

A problem with many agile methods is that they presume that self-organizing teams will also automatically incorporate the right processes and methods.

> **Note**
>
> For a discussion on the assumptions on self-organizing teams underlying many of the agile methods in the market, see *Cliff Berg: The Agile Community Embraces an Unworkable Fantasy*: `https://www.linkedin.com/pulse/agile-community-embraces-unworkable-fantasy-cliff-berg`. As Berg points out in this article, *"it is unreasonable to expect organizations to come up with Agile approaches just by learning the Agile Manifesto: they need help in defining new processes and practices, that over time will become the new normal"*.

The services model we have discussed is based on articulating processes and practices, and it is this feature of the service model that allows us to integrate security services with agile practices.

In this sense, explicitly articulating security services is the first step in developing a well-integrated security practice in the development and deployment cycle of new applications.

DevOps cycle

The DevOps cycle is usually sketched as an ouroboros (a snake eating its tail) in an infinity shape, as shown in the following diagram:

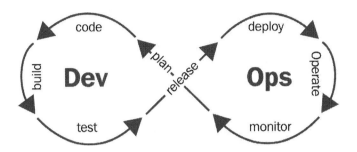

Figure 9.3 – The DevOps cycle

It is common to consider delivering security services in this development cycle as a process of DevSecOps, with the *Sec* stuck between the dev and the ops to stress that security is an integral part of the cycle and a key deliverable in its result.

The service architecture that we have discussed, which focuses on the strategy and products, policies, architecture, deployment, and ongoing monitoring, matches the various stages in this cycle:

- The strategy service matches the planning phase.

- The code and build phase matches the architecture service.

- Test, release, and deploy match the deployment service.

- Operate and monitor match the monitoring and alerting service.

The policies service and the incident response service are services that wrap around the entire cycle.

The advantage of addressing this problem in the language of services is that the manner in which a security team delivers security into the DevOps process becomes measurable and accountable.

Summary

In this chapter, we discussed structuring security operations as a set of services. This provides an advantage to the security teams as they can clearly articulate what they provide to the business and how. It also helps with understanding and working on the cadence of security operations.

Then, we discussed how to use the language of services to integrate agile and security operations so that security becomes part of development and operations in a way that is repeatable and measurable.

In the next chapter, which will be the last chapter of this book, we'll be looking at threat intelligence and how threat intelligence can be used in a security operations context.

10
Implementing Agile Threat Intelligence

Advanced security programs use threat-informed defense to power up their incident response and day-to-day defenses. This implies that these programs consume threat intelligence and have integrated threat intelligence with the rest of their security operations. This final chapter will deal with an approach to doing that.

Threat intelligence requires a significant amount of organizational readiness, as well as a mindset that's associated with agile. Threat intelligence (or intelligence proper) involves dealing with uncertainty, being wrong at times, taking calculated risks, and performing assessments that may only have a temporary value.

A credible threat intelligence program, which is a program in which intelligence is not only consumed, but also used, consists of several activities that are best performed in the context of agile security operations, such as curation, threat hunting, tasking, and adversary simulation.

This chapter will cover the following topics, which, when put together, describe the threat intelligence cycle:

- What threat intelligence is and isn't
- A threat intelligence program
- Direction
- Collection and collation
- Interpretation
- Dissemination

You may be wondering, what is agile about threat intelligence? Agile threat intelligence focuses on consuming and developing threat intelligence – that is, it's timely, actionable, and open to revision and adaption when the situation requires it. This requires agility in the threat intelligence program and agility among the people operating it.

What threat intelligence is and isn't

In the previous chapters of this book, we discussed how incident response is at the core of security practices. This is also true for threat intelligence. The closure of the incident response loop, which we discussed in *Chapter 3, Engineering for Incident Response*, allows us to sketch the placement of a cyber threat intelligence program into security operations.

As we discussed there, the result of this retrospective in incident response is intelligence, TTPs, and the context of the incident that was just resolved. Threat intelligence is the process of gathering structured, actionable information about attackers from our threats, as well as from outside sources.

The role of threat intelligence in closing the incident response process is shown in the following diagram:

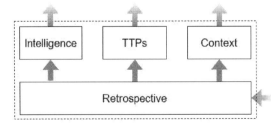

Figure 10.1 – The context of cyber threat intelligence

From the preceding diagram, it should be clear that threat intelligence is not just a firehose of threat data that's consumed indiscriminately – it requires context and processing to be of use to the organization. Threat intelligence, when done well, is hard work.

Context and threat intelligence processing is best described with the **intelligence cycle**, in which data is collected, curated, disseminated, and ultimately used. Cyber threat intelligence depends on this cycle, and the steps in the threat intelligence cycle form the components of a threat intelligence program.

The classic intelligence cycle consists of the following steps:

- **Direction**: The statement of the intelligence requirement. This should take the form of a specific question usually focused on a strategic or business problem.

- **Collection**: Defining and acquiring the essential information.

- **Collation**: All the essential elements from all the sources are collated into a readily accessible and searchable collection.

- **Interpretation**: Information is analyzed and turned into intelligence.

- **Dissemination**: The intelligence is communicated in written or oral form.

The purpose of a threat intelligence program is to improve the detection and prevention of attacks by using detailed knowledge about the toolset and behavior of the attacker.

> **The Threat Intelligence Cycle and Intelligence Failures**
>
> It should come as no surprise that intelligence failures are, in many cases, attributable to organizations making fatal mistakes in the various steps of the threat intelligence cycle. So, understanding the different steps and their implementation is key to having a better understanding of how threat intelligence may be consumed and processed. Examples of how intelligence failures may be attributable to failures in the intelligence cycle in classical intelligence have been collected in J. Hughes-Wilson, *On Intelligence: The History of Espionage and the Secret World*, Little, Brown Book Group, London, 2016.

The threat intelligence cycle is depicted in the following diagram. It shows the various stages that organizations must follow to use a cyber threat intelligence program:

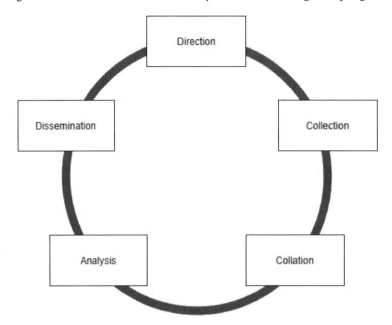

Figure 10.2 – The threat intelligence cycle

To this end, we can use the intelligence cycle shown in the preceding diagram while keeping in mind that the dissemination of the information is not entirely in written reports, but in actual inputs to detection and prevention – that is, tasking our infrastructure with that specific detection.

A threat intelligence program

How does the intelligence cycle fit with the entirety of the security program? In the context of what we discussed in *Chapter 7, How Secure Are You?– Measuring Security Posture*, threat intelligence is a capability that has strategic value, both for the security program as well as for the entire organization.

In the context of implementing threat intelligence, we will focus on acquiring threat intelligence from outside sources, and then also consider what is required to implement a threat intelligence program.

Acquiring threat intelligence

Commercial or community-based threat intelligence is usually provided in the form of feeds, which are formatted into a protocol that can be used to share threat intelligence, such as STIX and TAXII or MISP. Community feeds are usually shared under the **traffic light protocol**, which we discussed in *Chapter 1, How Security Operations Are Changing*. Commercial feeds also have commercial terms regarding their use and dissemination throughout the organization.

Threat intelligence can come in various types:

- **Strategic**: Strategic threat intelligence is intelligence at the level of the business or sector that the organization operates in. It consists of threat landscape surveys, threat reports for specific threat groups, or new and somewhat unknown varieties of compromise for business processes. Strategic threat intelligence lets the business make changes to its strategy and has long-term value.

- **Tactical**: Tactical threat intelligence focuses on the operations of specific threat groups, as well as the methods that are being used by threat groups to compromise their victims. Tactical threat intelligence is of medium-term value and allows an organization to design and deploy both detections and defenses, as well as enable threat hunting.

- **Operational**: Operational threat intelligence focuses on distributing indicators of compromise or specific FQDNs that are being used for malicious activities and allows an organization to deploy immediate low-level detections, usually at the bottom end of the pyramid of pain. The pyramid of pain is a classification scheme for indicators (it was also referenced in *Chapter 3, Engineering for Incident Response*, and *Chapter 6, Active Defense*).

Running your own function

Apart from accessing threat intelligence through an outside feed, it is also possible to form and operate an internal threat intelligence team, either as a part of incident response or as an entirely separate function in the security team.

A cyber threat intelligence program is based on the threat intelligence cycle but also incorporates some modifications to this cycle. As an example, we have the collection phase, which may involve the sort of activities that people associate with spying on traditional intelligence. In the cyber variety, it involves gathering data from intelligence sources, performing reconnaissance activities on adversaries, and using known patterns of attack from the ATT&CK matrix or similar sources.

In cyber threat intelligence, the collation and interpretation phases primarily focus on how to deal with large and complex data sources and may involve data mining and artificial intelligence to make sense of it all.

A team can start the threat intelligence function in a low-key manner once they close the incident loop in the manner discussed in *Chapter 3, Engineering for Incident Response*, and consider the threat-based improvements in their infrastructure. A team may then opt to share these findings with an outside group of organizations that they team up with and trust under the traffic light protocol, for instance.

Using threat intelligence

But the biggest modification that is made in cyber threat intelligence is in dissemination, which, in traditional intelligence terms, means writing a report and sharing it with the people that have been cleared to read that report. In cyber threat intelligence, while you may do such reporting, dissemination is also a key element of our old friend detection engineering, but its benefits are not limited to just that.

Specifically, the dissemination component focuses on *operationalizing* threat intelligence so that it becomes useful to the business. Operationalization can take three forms:

- **Detection engineering**, where the new intelligence is translated into specific detections that are then deployed.

- **Threat hunting**, where the new intelligence is used to inform hunt queries. Tactical threat intelligence is particularly useful in this scenario.

- **Infrastructure hardening**, where operational threat intelligence is deployed in static defenses to harden the infrastructure against those specific threats.

In this last scenario, dissemination involves **tasking** detection and prevention infrastructure with up-to-date indicators of compromise that have been collected through the intelligence program, so that it can detect or prevent the attack. This is a form of infrastructure hardening that makes it more resilient against attacks.

> **Note**
>
> On the first.org website, you can find a detailed course on threat intelligence: https://www.first.org/education/trainings#FIRST-Threat-intel-Pipelines-Course.

In terms of the intelligence cycle, in cyber threat intelligence, we must consider the following:

- **Direction**: The direction phase is guided by considering threats and risks to the organization, ranging from the activities of specific threat groups to the risks to the sector the business operates in.

- **Collection**: In the collection phase, we can consider traditional news sources for reports of attacks in our industry or sector, the outcome of our current security incidents, monitoring leaked enterprise accounts that appear in dumps, become part of a threat sharing group, or monitor the exploits of our most frequent vulnerabilities.

- **Collation**: All the essential elements from all the sources are collated into a readily accessible database, which is commonly called a threat intelligence platform. The collation process describes the process whereby all the elements that make up the intelligence product are put together in a form that allows analysis.

- **Interpretation**: In this phase, the information is analyzed and enriched by combining several elements. This is often a manual process, which can follow some of the techniques we discussed earlier for analyzing incidents.

- **Dissemination**: In this phase, the intelligence that's been collected is communicated in written or oral form to an audience. This may include organizational leadership, internal stakeholders, and external parties as required. This phase also involves looking at our defensive infrastructure through detection engineering.

In the remainder of this chapter, we will discuss these steps in more detail and outline operational procedures that describe how they can be implemented.

Direction

Running a threat intelligence program is hard and may be expensive. In *Chapter 7, How Secure Are You? – Measuring Security Posture*, we discussed the elements of a risk and strategy framework that allows the security posture of the business to be measured. In this section, we will apply that framework to threat intelligence collection.

The critical success factors for direction are as follows:

- Having a robust understanding of how impacts on capabilities and operations translate into business risk

- Realizing that past incidents are a partial, but not complete, guide to the future

- Combining threat modeling and business modeling into attack path modeling to understand the financial underpinnings of risk reduction

Let's now discuss the risk reduction strategies.

Understanding risk reduction

In terms of the risk framework, we are interested in the potential for threats to impact business operations and capabilities.

We discussed the strategy development model in *Chapter 7, How Secure Are You?–Measuring Security Posture*. This model also gives us a way to translate (qualitatively) the degradation of operations or capabilities into risks to the business by considering how such a degradation affects the various customers and their finances.

The following diagram shows how this model can degrade processes and capabilities and translate them into business risks:

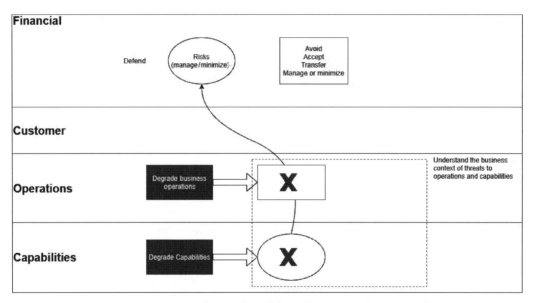

Figure 10.3 – Degradation of capabilities flowing into business risk

From this, it is clear that cyber defenders need to have robust insights into the key business processes and how they affect customers to develop a view regarding which threats would lead to the largest risks.

We can combine this understanding with our discussion of **use cases** from *Chapter 6, Active Defense*, to develop a good view of which particular use cases would be the most damaging to the business, and then focus on those.

Using past attacks as a guide

Another way to get a handle on direction is to close the incident loop and look at all past attacks, successful or not, as events that are likely to happen again in the future. This is *not* to say that past events form a *complete* guide to what may happen in the future. But past events provide a *partial* guide into the future – one where we may combine past experiences with our lessons learned to get better future outcomes.

Groups that have attacked us in the past, especially in cases where we have decided that they are advanced *persistent* groups, are likely to be back in the future, , with tactics and techniques that are variations on the ones used in the attacks we have already come across and resolved. Closing the incident loop means we are already familiar with those tactics and techniques and are more likely to recognize variations of them in the future.

Scoping prospective groups

In addition to the knowledge about attacks and attack groups that have already occurred, we can also scope prospective groups that are, for instance, active in our industry to get a view of who may attack us in the future. In *Chapter 6, Active Defense*, we discussed how we can use a combination of news feeds, threat intelligence platforms, and even indictments to map out new potential adversaries.

Business capabilities and operational context

Combining all this information should give us a decent overview of the most active threats for our organizations as well as the tactics, techniques, and, to some degree, procedures associated with those threats.

At this point, we must map these threats and their tactics to business capabilities and operations. Threats pose a risk because of their capability to disrupt or destroy capabilities and business processes, and it is in this sense that they pose a risk. In addition to these TTPs, the *impact* tactic in the last column of the ATT&CK framework (`https://attack.mitre.org/tactics/TA0040/`) can also help map the *impact* of threats, both real and perceived, to processes and capabilities.

By considering past attacks as well as prospective attacks, we can build a retrospective and prospective view of business risk.

In the *retrospective* view, we are certain about the impact that threat group will have on our infrastructure because we have been here before: the impact of the attacks from that group and their copycats will have been broadly known. However, we are uncertain that this group will be back. They may or may not.

In the *prospective* view, we have additional uncertainty about both the likelihood of the attack as well as its impact. Both retrospective and proactive views work together to establish an estimate of the threat landscape being faced by the organization.

The direction of cyber threat intelligence may also include information about our organization, how well they are organized, and the defenses that are already in place, all of which are evaluated against the assessment of the threat landscape.

The influence on direction

In the direction phase, the organization defines the objectives of its threat intelligence program: the intelligence it wants to collect and what it wants to do with it. The direction question, since it focuses on risk, can take several different forms:

- Which cyber threat adversaries are the most dangerous to our organization? Why?

- How well is our organization prepared to counter these threats? What does the environment look like from the viewpoint of a defender and the viewpoint of an attacker?

- What critical information would be required by the executive team to make decisions about responding to an incident, should the scenario outlined in the threat assessment eventuate?

The direction phase of a threat intelligence program is a strategic phase that is unique to each organization. Organizations need to organically consider threats and their impact on their systems and ask specific, directed, and answerable questions related to their threat intelligence program.

Collection and collation

Once the direction of threat intelligence has been established, we need to consider how the data is collected and treated so that it can answer the directive question(s).

Threat intelligence is usually made available as a feed, which contains information about various artifacts (usually somewhat down on the pyramid of pain) that constitute various degrees of threat to the organization. But feeding data like this is meaningless if it is not combined with a business context.

The data funnel

A concept that is useful for describing the process of generating threat intelligence in the business is depicted in the following diagram, which depicts a funnel where data originating in our own organization is progressively collected, put together, and analyzed:

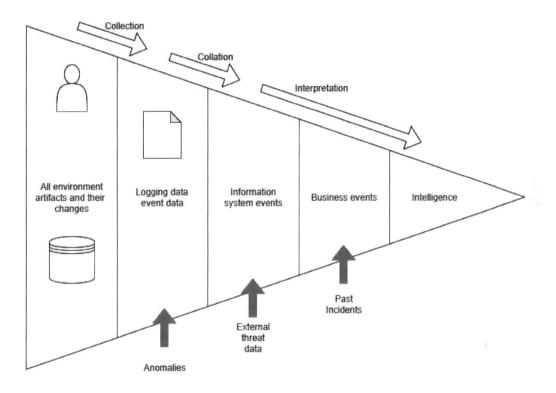

Figure 10.4 – The threat intelligence data funnel

In this model, the environment generates logging and event data, which is collected and collated (put together) in a single place and combined with a threat feed of known (usually lower level) indicators of malicious activity. The question then is whether, at some point, the information available from our logs matches the activity.

As we can also see from this diagram, external feeds are only one part of the possible threat intelligence that we have access to, with the other ones being anomalies and past incidents.

When anomalies are followed up consistently, we get to the practice of threat hunting, which aims to establish whether the observed anomalies are part of an existing threat by following some leads that have been generated by threat intelligence. We discussed threat hunting in *Chapter 8, Red, Blue, and Purple Teaming*.

We have already argued that past incidents provide a robust guide to the threats faced by our organization since we understand past events from the viewpoint of business impact, not just technical indicators. Closing the incident loop is all about ensuring that we obtain the most intelligence from past incidents and reuse them for future benefit.

External feeds

Threat intelligence vendors work hard to monitor the corners of the internet where we usually don't go, such as underground forums where attackers may go to exchange methods, victim information, or planned attacks. They then translate this information into early warnings for their customers. In addition, commercial threat feed vendors can feed us IOCs that are associated with threat groups.

Commercially available threat feeds can lead to a spigot of data, usually without much business context. As a rule, the feed data sits lower in the pyramid of pain, which we briefly mentioned in *Chapter 3, Engineering for Incident Response*.

It makes little sense to just go out and buy a threat feed. Some considerations for threat feeds are as follows:

- How specific is the threat feed with regard to our business environment, and does the information supplied by the vendor match with my understanding of the major risks my organization faces?
- Does the threat data usefully extend my understanding of those risks?
- Is the format that the data is supplied in consistent with the platform I am using to store my data?

I hope this model makes it clear that external threat feeds are important, but that they are by no means the only way of getting threat intelligence.

Feeds meeting internal logs

Feeds can be matched to log events to create **sightings**; positive confirmation of some bad actors on our network. Sightings should be further investigated as part of our incident response processes.

We also need to ensure that we log data that is meaningful in a threat intelligence context. To that end, we must devise a logging strategy, as discussed in *Chapter 3, Engineering for Incident Response*, and *Chapter 6, Active Defense*. Following the TTPs in the ATT&CK framework can assist in determining which events to log and how.

This stage of the threat intelligence program is not particularly different from the security practices we have already discussed in terms of its implementation. This changes once we get to the next stage.

Interpretation

Interpretation focuses on how to make sense of threat intelligence at the level of our IT systems as well as the business, and ultimately the threat groups and risks. Whereas most incident response practices focus on resolving the incidents, generating threat intelligence from incident data involves generalizing the observed data into a set of TTPs and evaluating those against the possible objectives of the attackers.

Using structured analytic techniques

The analytic tools we can use to do this are structured analytic techniques, which we have already mentioned in *Chapter 4, Key Concepts in Cyber Defense*. These structured analytic techniques can help us generate and test hypotheses that explain the observed data patterns and can assist us with generating the TTPs related to a specific attack.

This is not a simple process as it relies on trial and error, as well as flexibility in revising prior views. To get good threat intelligence, we need to have a good explanation of each event and robust analysis, which is not easy to come by.

Threat groups

Data from multiple attacks, once it's been collected and documented, can lead us to threat groups if we **cluster** the TTPs that we have observed. The idea behind this is that threat groups have a business model that states the things they know how to do best and most easily, as well as what characterizes an attack group is this business model alongside the objectives outlined. Some of the variables that influence attack clustering are as follows:

- The tactics and methodology followed by the group to compromise their victims. Some groups focus on phishing for credentials, while others specialize in malware-laden office documents.

- Imputed objectives: some groups are financially motivated, while others attempt to steal intellectual property or perform extortion.

- The industry segments that are targeted by a group.

- The malware families that are used by the group.

- The exploits that are used by a group.

It usually takes more than one attack to correctly characterize the threat group behind it, but especially for *persistent* threats, such efforts pay off impressively.

> **Note**
>
> An article discussing a clustering algorithm for threat groups can be found here: `https://www.fireeye.com/blog/threat-research/2019/03/clustering-and-associating-attacker-activity-at-scale.html`. This is one of the many ways in which you can cluster groups.

Clustering is sometimes made more difficult because of certain threat groups only specializing in some aspects of intrusion, where the results are then sold to other groups. Access brokers, for instance, specialize in gaining access to victims but may sell this access to other groups.

In other cases, common malware is sold to anyone who is considering becoming a bad actor on the internet, so it is not uncommon to see such malware in use across several groups at the same time.

Both trends make clustering harder, which is why it can take multiple years and large amounts of attack data before a trustworthy assignment can be made.

There is no standard terminology for candidate threat groups, with Mandiant using the *UNC* prefix and Microsoft using the *DEV* prefix. Once the attack groups have been categorized, however, the common prefixes for the group names are *ATP* for advanced persistent threat and *FIN* for financially motivated groups. At the time of writing, many ransomware gangs, if they have been classified, are in the FIN category.

Dissemination

Disseminating cyber threat intelligence focuses on how we use the result of the threat intelligence exercise. It can occur in various forms.

The extended data funnel for threat intelligence, as outlined in the following diagram, mentions a few components: risk analysis, alerting, detection engineering, and tasking. In the following diagram, we are not representing the external threat feeds as a specific input:

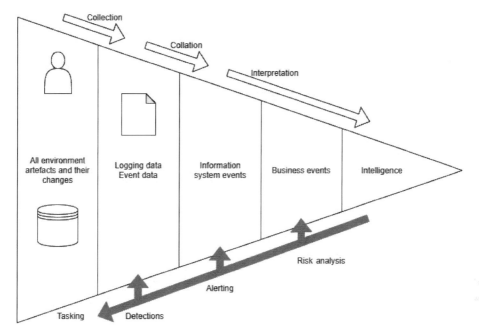

Figure 10.5 – Closing the threat intelligence loop

These three elements play out at different levels of the organization. Risk analysis focuses on the strategic aspect of security operations and considers the impact on the business. Alerting, detection engineering, and tasking play out at the tactical level of security operations.

Risk analysis

Intelligence about threat groups can be used by assessing the cost to the business concerning the typical impacts that result from that group, alongside the TTPs, to establish the risk this group poses to our organization.

From our discussion in *Chapter 1*, *How Security Operations Are Changing*, we know that risk is the combination of a threat event, which we can get a handle on with cyber threat intelligence, our vulnerability, and the impact caused by the event (*Figure 1.1* and the surrounding discussion). A cyber threat intelligence program allows us to correctly estimate the risks that are posed by the threat groups that are active in our sector.

Alerting, hunting, and detection

Having a good handle on the threat groups that are active in our environment allows us to design a better alerting and detection framework that takes this knowledge into account.

Detection

We have already discussed the practice of detection engineering, which amounts to treating detections as code that need to be continuously updated so that the improvements stay relevant to the user. A cyber threat intelligence program provides the direction for that process by outlining which threat actors are relevant, what their TTPs look like, and what these threat actors look like early in the kill chain.

In this way, we can develop and continuously improve detections for these actors that catch them early rather than later.

The threat intelligence input to detection engineering can take different forms:

- **Indicators of compromise (IOCs)**, which consist of specific file hashes, FQDNs, IP addresses, packet signatures, or other low-level threat data that can be put into detection tooling almost directly.

- Collections of this data, such as in a sigma rule, which can be processed programmatically to be deployed into detection infrastructure or the SIEM.

- Tactical threat intelligence, which usually leads to the development of new detections. To go from tactical intelligence to new detections, you need to consider how this tactic or technique may be detected or prevented.

> **Sigma Rules**
>
> Sigma rules are generic rules that describe the signatures of threats and how they can be detected in general, so that the rules become portable between systems. A converter program can be used to translate these sigma rules into the specific formats that are used by a SIEM or log aggregation platform:
>
> `https://github.com/SigmaHQ/sigma`.

Threat hunts

Threat intelligence information can also be used in the case of threat hunts. Threat intelligence information allows us to search our past data and logs with the help of specific intelligence-driven hunt leads: analytic queries to look for evidence of the presence of the group we have received intelligence about.

Hunting is best deployed in combination with tactical threat intelligence, which involves focusing on the tactics of the group that is the hunt target to ensure that its chosen techniques and procedures can be detected and mitigated.

Infrastructure hardening

One of the most interesting results that can flow from a threat intelligence program is the capability to harden our infrastructure with the specific technical indicators that are associated with the threat groups that we want to protect our organization against.

It is a great bonus to be able to be specific about such groups, rather than having to deploy every potential indicator related to all groups. The latter approach is likely to overwhelm our infrastructure and processes, long before it even finishes, as blocklists become longer, data is loaded indiscriminately, and we have a non-existent process for weeding out stale data from the blocklist.

Some considerations and key questions to ask when considering this hardening are as follows:

- Automation is essential but needs to be driven by judicious discrimination in what to load, lest we overwhelm the system.

- Loading data is as important as unloading data. We cannot afford a situation where blocklists just get indiscriminately longer and longer.

- The timeliness of the data. It makes no sense to block URLs and hashes that were relevant, say, 2 weeks ago, but are no longer used by the attackers..

Like everything we have discussed in this book, creating, developing, and using threat intelligence is a cycle of continuous improvement that requires the agile processes to undergo rapid feedback and incremental improvement.

Summary

In this final chapter, we discussed creating, consuming, and utilizing threat intelligence to strengthen an already existing program so that it can perform threat-informed defense. Threat-informed defense is driven by having a robust program for performing incident management and extracting intelligence from incident data, as well as observations, engineered detections, and actions.

A point we have not discussed in this chapter, but one that is worth mentioning is that a well-executed threat intelligence program can significantly improve the standing of security operations at an executive level, where people deal with risks. Threat intelligence, when done well, makes such risks not only quantifiable but also visible.

Appendix

Principles of cybersecurity operations

In my earlier book, *Principles of Cyber Security Operations*, I laid out seven principles for effective cyber security defense. In this appendix, I enumerate the principles and give a brief explanation.

The principles are as follows:

1. *Visibility: Go by what there is, not by what there should be*: Look at your own environment like an intruder would. This means discovering and seeing for yourself what there is on your network, using the same tooling (with limitations) that an intruder would use, testing, improving, and testing again.

2. *Visibility has its limits*: Ensure the security team does not have access to everything. Security should have enough access to things to do their jobs, no more.

3. *Context: Close the Incident Loop*: Don't just be content with recovering from an incident. See what you can learn, and, more importantly, what you can improve.

4. *Share aggressively*: Security is teamwork. There is no competitive value in keeping attack data to yourself.

5. *Do not become a risk yourself*: Ensure that your team uses good security around their own operations. This is for two reasons: security works better if it is road-tested by us first, and the security team is an attractive target.

6. *Do not start a battle on all fronts*: Develop an approach that reduces the real risks to an organization, rather than trying to fix everything at once. At the same time, also choose battles you can win. Success breeds success.

7. *Strategy's essence*: The essence of a good security strategy is a deep understanding of the business, the security events that have already occurred, and those that may occur. The strategy then connects this understanding to actions that improve matters.

Further reading

This book has covered a lot of ground, and if you are setting up an agile security operations practice, there is more to cover still.

This appendix collects some useful resources on which the thinking in this book is based, as well as suggestions for places where you might go for more information.

Background

Cynefin framework

Dave Snowden, Riva Greenberg, Boudewijn Bertsch, Sue Borchardt, Sonja Blignaut, and Zhen Goh: *Cynefin – Weaving Sense-Making into the Fabric of Our World Cognitive Edge* – The Cynefin Co., (2020): `https://www/cognitive-edge.com/cynefinbook/`.

A large number of resources and further references are available at

`www.cynefin.io`.

You can also follow Dave Snowden's blog at `https://www.cognitive-edge.com/author/dave-snowden/`.

Cynefin Field guide

This book makes several references to the field guide for managing complexity and chaos in times of crisis.

Snowden, D. and Rancati, A., *Managing complexity (and chaos) in times of crisis. A field guide for decision makers inspired by the Cynefin® framework*, Publications Office of the European Union, Luxembourg, 2020, JRC123629

A copy is available here:

`https://publications.jrc.ec.europa.eu/repository/handle/JRC123629`

Structured analytic techniques

Richards, J. Heuer and Randolph H. Pherson: *Structured Analytic Techniques for Intelligence Analysis*, Third Edition, SAGE, 2020

Architecture

Ed Moyle, Diana Kelley: *Practical Cybersecurity Architecture*, Packt, November 2020

Threat modeling

Adam Shostack: *Threat Modeling: Designing for Security*, Wiley, 2014

Organizations

NIST makes available a vast library of resources for standards, architecture, operations, and incident response. The NIST cybersecurity framework ties it all together and the NIST framework page is a good starting point to explore what is available:

`https://www.nist.gov/cyberframework`.

The MITRE corporation (`https://www.mitre.org/`) maintains the ATT&CK framework, the center for threat informed defense, as well as a large number of other initiatives focusing on cybersecurity operations, supported by open source software (`https://github.com/mitre`). These pages can change frequently, and it is a good idea to check back for the latest version.

`https://www.first.org/` is focused on incident response and practices in security teams and publishes standards and training.

SANS is an organization focused on education and training (`https://www.sans.org/apac/`).

Operations

Principles for operations

Hinne Hettema: *Principles for Cybersecurity Operations*, CreateSpace, 2020

SOC operations

The following resource is indispensable if you are setting up a security operational capability.

Jason Zimmerman: *Ten Strategies of a World Class SOC*, Mitre Corporation, 2014

```
https://www.mitre.org/publications/all/ten-strategies-of-a-
world-class-cybersecurity-operations-center
```

People to follow

The following is a list of people who regularly publish material in relation to security operations along the lines we have discussed in this book. This list is far from complete but forms a starting point from which you can quickly grow your own list of people to follow on Twitter and social media:

- Rob van Os: `https://soc-cmm.com/`.

- Anton Chuvakin: `http://www.chuvakin.org/`

- Mehmet Ergene (@Cyb3rMonk): `https://mergene.medium.com/`

- Florian Roth (@cyb3rops): `https://twitter.com/Cyb3rOps`

My suggestion is that you take this as a starting point and curate your own list of resources to follow on social media and blogs to stay on point with what happens in security.

Index

E

Packt.com

Subscribe to our online digital library for full access to over 7,000 books and videos, as well as industry leading tools to help you plan your personal development and advance your career. For more information, please visit our website.

Why subscribe?

- Spend less time learning and more time coding with practical eBooks and Videos from over 4,000 industry professionals

- Improve your learning with Skill Plans built especially for you

- Get a free eBook or video every month

- Fully searchable for easy access to vital information

- Copy and paste, print, and bookmark content

Did you know that Packt offers eBook versions of every book published, with PDF and ePub files available? You can upgrade to the eBook version at packt.com and as a print book customer, you are entitled to a discount on the eBook copy. Get in touch with us at customercare@packtpub.com for more details.

At www.packt.com, you can also read a collection of free technical articles, sign up for a range of free newsletters, and receive exclusive discounts and offers on Packt books and eBooks.

Other Books You May Enjoy

If you enjoyed this book, you may be interested in these other books by Packt:

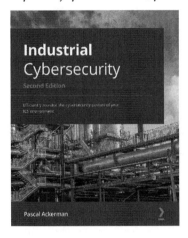

Industrial Cybersecurity - Second Edition

Pascal Ackerman

ISBN: 9781800202092

- Monitor the ICS security posture actively as well as passively

- Respond to incidents in a controlled and standard way

- Understand what incident response activities are required in your ICS environment

- Perform threat-hunting exercises using the Elasticsearch, Logstash, and Kibana (ELK) stack

- Assess the overall effectiveness of your ICS cybersecurity program

- Discover tools, techniques, methodologies, and activities to perform risk assessments for your ICS environment

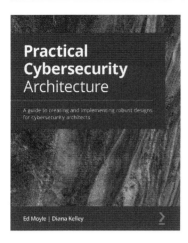

Practical Cybersecurity Architecture

Ed Moyle, Diana Kelley

ISBN: 9781838989927

- Explore ways to create your own architectures and analyze those from others
- Understand strategies for creating architectures for environments and applications
- Discover approaches to documentation using repeatable approaches and tools
- Delve into communication techniques for designs, goals, and requirements
- Focus on implementation strategies for designs that help reduce risk
- Become well-versed with methods to apply architectural discipline to your organization

Packt is searching for authors like you

If you're interested in becoming an author for Packt, please visit `authors.packtpub.com` and apply today. We have worked with thousands of developers and tech professionals, just like you, to help them share their insight with the global tech community. You can make a general application, apply for a specific hot topic that we are recruiting an author for, or submit your own idea.

Share Your Thoughts

Now you've finished *Agile Security Operations*, we'd love to hear your thoughts! Scan the QR code below to go straight to the Amazon review page for this book and share your feedback or leave a review on the site that you purchased it from.

https://packt.link/r/1801815518

Your review is important to us and the tech community and will help us make sure we're delivering excellent quality content.

Made in the USA
Monee, IL
12 November 2022

17640987R00140